'What a helpful, engaging, and God honoring book! Knowing it will help marriages at any stage, I will highly recommend "The Diamond Marriage" to my congregation and to others with whom I speak.'

Joel C. Hunter, Senior Pastor, Northland Church, Florida

'This is a well informed book and constructively addresses crucial questions which many other marriage books tend to neglect.'

Ann Benton, author of 'Don't they make a Lovely Couple' and 'Aren't They Lovely When They're Asleep?'

'Here is a monumental work of love and energy, from one of the most effective Christian ministers in the UK. Today, when the foundations of marriage are under attack from outside and within the church, "The Diamond Marriage" comes as a book that is timely and urgently needed among us all.'

Richard Bewes OBE, author of 'Top 100 Questions' and 'Words that Circled the World'

'This is a truly excellent book. I warmly commend The Diamond Marriage for its practical wisdom and theological insight into the ultimate purpose of Christian Marriage. I encourage you to read it and work through the practical exercises aimed at reviving healthy and god-glorifying marriages which will be invaluable at a time when marriage is under unprecedented assault from all sides. Simon has done us a great service.'

Wallace Benn, Bishop of Lewes

'Dr Vibert has written an excellent book on marriage and marriage relationships. This work is sensitive, challenging, and born out of a clear biblical understanding of the subject matter combined with a wealth of pastoral experience. I warmly recommend it.'

Paul Gardner, Archdeacon of Exeter

'This practical and scholarly book will be a help and encouragement to many couples. It has a refreshing emphasis on joy and delight in marriage. And it is heartening to read such a thoughtful treatment of the husband's calling to Christlike headship and the wife's to Christian submission, written in a way which relates these realistically to the contemporary world.'

Christopher Ash, Director, Cornhill Training Course
author of 'Marriage: Sex in the service of God'

'What another book on Christian marriage? Having lectured on marriage counselling for the past nineteen years my bookshelves already contain a good selection on marriage. So why would I want to buy this one?

Books on Christian marriage tend to fall into two categories. Some are practical "self-help" manuals using biblical passages to "fix" the relationship. Others are more theological but with little sensible help with day-to-day issues. Simon successfully combines the two. This book challenges you to think about marriage from a theological perspective, looking at marriage in a fuller context in relation to God and his purposes for marriage. It helpfully applies those insights into the practicalities of married life.

Here is a great challenge to living marriage as God intended it to be – joyfully and honouring to God, and not to be content with merely doing our duty. Very readable with great touches of humour – well worth adding to the bookshelves!

Rev. Clare Hendry
Minister of Pastoral Care, St James' Church, Muswell Hill
Formerly Lecturer in Pastoral Counselling,
Oak Hill Theological College

THE

DIAMOND

MARRIAGE

*Have Ultimate Purpose
in your Marriage*

Simon Vibert

CHRISTIAN FOCUS

© Simon Vibert, 2005

1-84550-076-8

10 9 8 7 6 5 4 3 2 1

Published in 2005
by
Christian Focus Publications, Ltd.
Geanies House, Fearn, Tain,
Ross-shire, IV20 1TW, Great Britain.

www.christianfocus.com

Cover Design by Moose77 Designs

Printed and bound by
Nørhaven Paperback A/S, Denmark

CONTENTS

To Caroline,

my complementary counterpart
and partner in our enacted parable.

My gratitude also goes to the staff at Reformed Theological Seminary in Orlando, and to Dr John Piper of Bethlehem Baptist Church Minneapolis for all that he taught me about Jonathan Edwards.

PREFACE

Do we really need another book on marriage? Christian and non-Christian books on husband/wife relationships are reaching near epidemic proportions. Without wishing to fire all my guns at this point, I should explain that I write as a husband, as a Christian, as a pastor and as a Bible teacher. I am not primarily concerned about the husband and wife relationship – yes, this book does have a lot to say about that subject, but only secondarily. My main task is to pose the question: 'What is the chief, or ultimate, end of marriage?' I am not just asking, 'In what way should God be involved in marriage?' Rather, my question is, 'Why has God gone to such great lengths to make marriage as we know it?' or 'What is the purpose of marriage?'

This is a daunting task! There are two subjects which are likely to bring shame and humiliation on the author: one source of embarrassment would be to write on prayer, the other would be to write on marriage. For, in both of these areas, the author is painfully aware of his own shortcomings. Actually, it could be argued that to write on marriage is likely to bring even more embarrassment than if one were to write on prayer, for at least shortcomings in prayer, for the most part, are only known to GOD!! However, my wife is very aware of how much I fail as a husband but, mercifully, and rather like God, she loves me even though she has come to know me through and through!

There is, in fact, a closer link between marriage and prayer than might at first be thought. In 1 Corinthians 7:5, Paul states that prayer is a good reason for abstinence and sexual discipline in the marriage relationship. But, only for a short time, after which, the couple should come back together.

There is one final justification for writing this book. It is that I write as a fellow marriage practitioner! I experience the joys and difficulties of marriage. But, most of all, I can write with the confidence that God has spoken with clarity and practical wisdom about the subject. After all, marriage was his idea in the first place, and he has not left us in the dark, but rather speaks clearly in his word.

So what follows is a book based almost exclusively on one text from the Bible, Genesis 2:24. And, though my failures be many, I am confident that a theologically applied explanation of this text will, I hope under God, be used to build your marriage – and maybe even your prayer life too!

ꟿNTRODUCTION

It was a wonderful occasion. The happy couple gathered all the family around them to celebrate their diamond wedding anniversary. Inspired by the occasion, the elderly husband called for a moment of hush, as he raised his glass to his wife, 'My darling, after sixty years of marriage I can tell all my family and friends that I have found you to be tried and true!' An approving murmur settled across the room. His wife lent forward on her stick, cupped her hand to her ear and said, 'Eh?'

Patiently, the husband repeated, 'My darling, after sixty years of marriage I can tell all my family and friends that I have found you tried and true!' Another murmur of approval. But the wife shouted in a loud voice, 'What?'

Rather louder, and a little less patiently, the husband said, 'After sixty years of marriage I have found you tried and true!' 'Huh,' replied the wife, 'and I can tell you that after sixty years of marriage I am sick and tired of you too!'

By anyone's reckoning, to reach a Diamond Wedding Anniversary is quite an achievement. It is hardly necessary to cite the current divorce statistics to make the point. However, I have been very struck by the fact that a recent Barna report[1] discovered that the national divorce rate stands at about 34 percent. While the divorce rates among those who claim to be Christian stands at 33 percent. Apparently, even holding Christian convictions does not reduce the incidence of divorce.

With those statistics in mind, we might be surprised to discover how many people still believe that marriage is a good idea and enter into it – once, indeed maybe several times!

One glorious Friday afternoon I met up with a friend to play nine holes of golf at my local course. The first hole is pretty easy. It is only 127 yards. I am sure that it is designed to break you in gently. Even despite this fact, I was left amazed by the first stroke played by the person in front of me.

He struck the ball well, it curved nicely and headed straight for the green. The ball plopped a few yards away from the hole, gently stopping and teetering on the edge of the hole, less than an inch away. I tell you, even though it was *someone else's* shot, it was still very exciting!

My first shot was rather less spectacular. However, the game went on. A few holes later I bumped into a guy who had given me a few golf lessons. He is a tested, professional golfer. With excitement, I told him about the first shot which had been played in front of me. With a twinkle in his eye, and not a little cynicism, he said to me, 'The only problem with a first shot like that is that you know that your game is going down hill from then on!'

The following day, a Saturday, I was taking the wedding of a long-standing church couple. There were any number of parallels which I could have drawn between the game of golf and marriage, but I resisted. What I did say to them was that so many people's view of marriage is rather like the comment my golf instructor made about that first golf shot. It all starts on the most amazing high – beautiful flowers, beautiful dress, beautiful bride, beautiful service and beautiful reception.

And, if the couple are fortunate, they're off on a wonderful honeymoon.

Then they come down to earth with a bump. It goes downhill from then on. They come back to their job, their mortgage, the familiarity of everyday life and slowly the reality sets in, and the initial joy and enthusiasm of marriage fades away.

This is a common perception of marriage. But is this scenario avoidable? It certainly seems that even today's Christians are less convinced that they should stick together 'till death do us part'. Divorce rates among Christian couples almost match those of non-Christian couples.

What Motivated Me to Study this Topic

As pastor of an evangelical church in London, I frequently come across Christian couples for whom marriage has become a faithful, but joyless, fulfilment of duty. There has been no adultery or unfaithfulness, but the marriage does not reflect the love that Christ has for the church (Eph. 5:21-32).

Most Christians take seriously the covenantal/contractual commitment made in the sight of God. Traditionally, this assumes that the married couple have become 'one flesh', and what 'God has joined together' should not be separated. Increasingly, couples in such situations are not persisting in their marriage and conclude that their marriage has lost its love, and divorce often ensues. It appears that, while a dutiful acceptance of biblical principles has been sufficient to keep marriages together in the past, Christian couples are no longer staying together when the display of joy in the marriage is absent.

This familiar scenario led me to ask whether we should be happy with such a view of Christian marriage. Why are many

Christian marriages dutiful but joyless? What has led us to be content with such an understanding of Christian love in marriage?

Part of the problem is revealed in a lack of adequate definition of *agapē* love. I sat in another church congregation last Sunday and heard a typical exposition of the biblical view of love. The preacher stated, when the passage uses the word *agapē* it does not mean 'feeling love, but action love'. This is an insufficient understanding of the word. Indeed, perhaps part of the problem in the Ephesian church which we are about to look at, is precisely this problem of defining love as if it had nothing to do with emotions and feelings.

The Ephesian Church – Dutiful but Loveless

Revelation 2:1–7

1 'To the angel of the church in Ephesus write: These are the words of him who holds the seven stars in his right hand and walks among the seven golden lampstands:

2 I know your deeds, your hard work and your perseverance. I know that you cannot tolerate wicked men, that you have tested those who claim to be apostles but are not, and have found them false.

3 You have persevered and have endured hardships for my name, and have not grown weary.

4 Yet I hold this against you: You have forsaken your first love.

5 Remember the height from which you have fallen! Repent and do the things you did at first. If you do not repent, I will come to you and remove your lamp stand from its place.

6 But you have this in your favour: You hate the practices of the Nicolaitans, which I also hate.

7 He who has an ear, let him hear what the Spirit says to the churches. To him who overcomes, I will give the right to eat from the tree of life, which is in the paradise of God.

Ephesus was a grand and proud city. At one time it was the commercial centre of Asia. The patron saint was the goddess Diana. Her image graced the trinket shops around the town (presumably, not controlled by royal copyright!).

When the apostle Paul began preaching in this city, there was such a dramatic impact that the idolatrous practices – and sale of such idols – immediately sent the town into turmoil (see Acts 19 for the details).

Several decades later, the apostle John writes to this church. Apparently, they have not waned in their hatred of idolatry, and Jesus has much to commend them for. But, as we shall see in a moment, their very zeal in certain areas has led to condemnation from Jesus too.

First, we notice, the Ephesians are commended for their intolerant zeal (vv. 2–3). They are not like those nauseating, lukewarm Laodiceans (Rev. 3:16). No! They are red hot, disciplined, faithful disciples. In particular, they hate the idolatrous practices of the Nicolaitans. We are not exactly sure what those practices were, but they seem to include a kind-of spiritual adultery – mixing beliefs and combining them with sexual immorality. But the Ephesians were to have none of that. Today, we might call the Ephesians narrow-minded fundamentalists! But Jesus commends them for their intolerant, steadfast loyalty to God.

But this is not the whole story. Jesus also has words of condemnation. His words are a very sad indictment on the church: 'Yet I hold this against you: You have forsaken your first love' (Rev. 2:4). In their zeal for the honour of God's name, their love for Jesus himself has grown cold. Or, to change the imagery, like many marriages, the couple have resisted the enticement of immorality and adultery but, sadly, the marriage has gone cold.

Sometimes a severe storm can blow over the apparently most sturdy of trees. Other times the tree seems to withstand all of that, but mysteriously whithers and dies – only after it has fallen, does it become apparent that the inside has been eaten away by disease.

The church at Ephesus has become like that tree. The joy of the Lord is absent. Sure, there is still discipline and a fighting for the cause of truth, but love has long gone. In particular, it seems as though the Ephesians are condemned, not so much for a lack of love for each other, but because their first love, love of the Lord himself, has gone cold.

Three issues arise from this brief look at Revelation 2 which relate to some modern marriage problems:

- Many people define love as disinterested actions rather than feelings.
- Many people assume that duty is more important than joy, which may be leading married couples to either despair of recapturing joy in their marriage, or resigning themselves to a marriage relationship which falls far short of the biblical ideal.
- Many Christian people have lost an appreciation of God's ultimate purpose for marriage. This lost perspective means that many couples do not see their relationship worked out in the light of God's ultimate purpose for marriage. (More on this later)

Risk Assessment Discussion

A recent, compulsory requirement, for charities in England is to undertake a risk assessment analysis. We held a church council meeting to discuss this subject. We tried to list the kinds of risks which we might face which could bring about financial ruin. We had to decide whether the risks had a high, medium or low probability of occurring. We then had to decide the likely impact these risks would have, should they occur.

The brainstorming revealed a number of familiar problems, such as loss of key staff workers; death of significant financial contributors, the impact of nuclear holocaust or earthquake! One wise gentleman on the council pointed out that the thing which could be considered both high probability and high impact would be 'a loss of vision, or complacency by the congregation'.

Our discussion was immediately reshaped. Our prime problems as a church do not come from the outside, but rather from within. And, they are also more subtle problems, problems which creep in, rather than attack you with the ferocity and aggression of a storm.

How true this is for marriage too! The problems faced by the Ephesian church in Revelation 2 relate to marriage, as well as to our relationship with God. In marriage, the chief risks consist of the loss of joy and the loss of one's first love, rather than sickness, adultery or financial ruin, serious those these issues are. Moreover, though subtle, the problem of complacency or loss of first love, is endemic, even in Christian marriages.

Confronted by the problem of failed Christian marriages, what can the church do about it? How can joy in marriage be revived? Could it be that joy in marriage is part of a more general joylessness in the Christian life?

My research on this issue led me to explore the question: 'How can I, as a husband and church pastor, help revive joy among Christian couples?'

Perhaps I can tell you a little about my own journey to this point, and the people who have influenced me along the way. There are three people who have helped change me from a typical English Stoic, to a person who believes that matters of the heart are integral, not only to a healthy marriage, but to a healthy relationship with God.

John Piper

John Piper is a prolific author. His most famous book is called *Desiring God*.

He recalls the famous first question of the Westminster Shorter Catechism. 'What is the chief end of man?' to which the traditional answer is: 'To glorify God and enjoy Him forever'. Piper argues, this statement feels a bit weak, as if the enjoyment of God is an added extra to glorifying God. It would be better to answer the question: 'The chief end of man is to glorify God *by* enjoying Him forever'.[2]

The significance of this change in wording is to signal the fact that we enjoy things that we truly value highly. This is essential in the realm of glorifying God too, and is not an added extra.

If you think about it for a moment, this statement about man's chief end, could also be applied to God himself. In his book *The Pleasures of God* (1991), Piper points out that God does everything to bring himself pleasure. Indeed 'God's chief end is to glorify God and enjoy himself forever.' God takes delight in his Son; he has so made creation to bring him pleasure and glory; he sovereignly elects, so that peoples from every nation will come to bring him glory. Indeed God does all things for his own pleasure.[3]

The reason you exist is to bring glory to God by making God your highest delight and your first love. The liberating thing about this truth is that your desire for happiness is not at odds with your quest for God. God wants us to find our chief end in God and our highest delight in God.

Piper illustrates the point as follows: Suppose it is my wedding anniversary. I return from work with a beautiful bouquet of two dozen red roses. My wife falls into my arms and exclaims, 'Simon, they are beautiful, you really shouldn't have!' I immediately stop her and retort, 'No, don't thank me, this is just what is expected of me on our wedding anniversary, I am just doing my duty – don't thank me, m'am, I'm just doing my job!'

Well, any romantic moment has immediately been deflated by such a comment! However, if I reply, 'My darling, I love you, and nothing gives me greater pleasure than to give you these roses', she will know that my motivation glorifies her and dignifies the moment. She is not going to turn to me and say, 'Simon, what is the matter with you? This moment is not about *your* pleasure and joy.' She knows that by finding my joy in this act, I am showing how much I honour her.

Consider the following scriptural passages:

> Delight yourself in the Lord and he will give you desires of your heart (Ps. 37:4).
>
> Rejoice in the Lord always, I will say it again, Rejoice (Phil. 4:4).
>
> God loves a cheerful giver (2 Cor. 9:7).

John Piper comments:

> Sin is pursuing happiness where it cannot be lastingly found (Jeremiah 2:12ff.), or pursuing it in the right direction, but with lukewarm, half-hearted affections (Revelation 3:16). Virtue, on the other hand, is to do what we do with all our might in pursuit of the enjoyment of all that God is for us in Jesus ... My discovery is that God is supreme not where he is simply served with duty but where he is savoured with delight.[4]

Already, we can see that John Piper's teaching helps address the question of dutiful but joyless marriages. But, Piper isn't the first to have taught this, and I think he is right to see it in scripture. C. S. Lewis has been a strong influence on him, especially in the things which Lewis has to say about the matter of praise.

C. S. Lewis

Lewis comments he had noticed that just as men spontaneously praise whatever they value, so they spontaneously urge us to join them in praising.

> The Psalmists in telling everyone to praise God are doing what all men do when they speak of what they care about ... I think we delight to praise what we enjoy because the praise not merely expresses but completes the enjoyment; it is its appointed consummation. It is not out of compliment that lovers keep on telling one another how beautiful they are; the delight is incomplete till it is expressed.[5]

In his essay, 'The Weight of Glory', Lewis comments that the problem with most of us is that we are more likely to be too stoical in our emotional reactions to God, rather than overemotional:

> If we consider the unblushing promises of reward and the staggering nature of the rewards promised in the Gospels, it would seem that our Lord finds our desires not too strong, but too weak. We are half-hearted creatures, fooling about with drink and sex and ambition when infinite joy is offered us, like an ignorant child who wants to go on making mud pies in a slum, because he cannot imagine what is meant by the offer of a holiday at the sea. We are far too easily pleased.[6]

Jonathan Edwards

Far more influential on John Piper's theology, and on mine too, is the writing of Jonathan Edwards, the eighteenth-century New England Puritan. One writer has commented on Jonathan Edwards' preaching as follows:

> For us to see Jonathan Edwards ascend his pulpit today, a candle in one hand and his sermon manuscript in the other, would cause a titter in the congregation. From our modern foam-cushioned church seats, with carpeted aisles and soothing background music, we can scarcely capture the old-time dignity of the unpretentious church where Edwards and others held captive the hearts and minds of their hearers.
>
> When Jonathan Edwards 'uttered' in the Spirit, the expressionless face, the sonorous voice, the sober clothing were forgotten. He was neither a dullard nor a sluggard. His was a devoted heart intent on rightly dividing the word of truth. But in doing it, Edwards flamed.[7]

Edwards made a number of resolutions in his life, one of which was:

> Resolved, to endeavour to obtain for myself as much happiness in the other world as I possibly can, with all the power, might, vigour and vehemence, yea, violence, I am capable of, or can bring myself to exert, in any way that can be thought of.[8]

He observes that true religion is religion of the heart:

> The religion which God requires, and will accept, does not consist in weak, dull and lifeless wishes, raising us but a little above a state of indifference: God, in His word, greatly insists upon it, that we be in good earnest, 'fervent in spirit,' and our hearts vigorously engaged in religion...[9]

This contrasts with the dangers of a hard heart, or a heart which has lost its first love:

> Now by a hard heart is plainly meant an unaffected heart, or a heart not easy to be moved with virtuous affections, like a stone, insensible, stupid, unmoved, and hard to be impressed. Hence the hard heart is called a *stony heart*, and is opposed to a heart of flesh, that has feeling, and is sensibly touched and moved.[10]

We will hear a bit more from each of these three men as we progress through the book. My point here is, if we are going to revive warm-hearted, joyful marriages, we must not be indifferent to our feelings. I am sure that we are agreed that feelings can mislead, and we should not live by feelings alone. But we certainly shouldn't go to the opposite extreme and assume that emotion, enthusiasm and delight is restricted to the Oval or Twickenham or Wembley. That which is most worthy of our worship is *most* worthy of our whole being, heart, soul, and mind, as Jesus' summary of the law asserts (see Mark 12:30). Similarly, if true love is to be shown in marriage, then, the heart must be moved by passion and joy.

What is the Cure?

So what is the answer for the church (or marriage) which is zealous but loveless?

The answer to this question is found in Revelation 2. Jesus called the Ephesian church to return to its first love. Many of the principles for restoring love towards God apply equally to the restoration of dutiful but joyless marriages:

Remember

Remember what it was that first incited love for the Lord. A loveless marriage would do well to get out the wedding video; to recount times together eating leisurely meals; talking about issues of the heart; or doing something especially for their own relationship.

Do you remember your first love? Was it not true that you did not need to *do* anything together, you simply wanted to *be* with each other. You wanted to spend every waking moment in each other's presence. Just ask your parents to remind you of the cost of the phone bill when they had teenagers in the house!

Is my joy in God? Is he my highest delight? I suggest that when you first believed, he was. Similarly, is your first love – not your football, your mates, your gym, your children or grandchildren – but your spouse? Everything else has its place, but, only after we remember our first love. In later chapters we will consider how this 'first love' can be rekindled in marriage.

Repent

Repentance is both saying and being sorry. It is a change of attitude which leads to a change in direction. I think of a clergy friend who, for the sake of his marriage, had to completely reorganize the way in which the vicarage was used by the parish. He moved meetings away from the home – and made sure he didn't go to all of them – so that he could give his family the time they needed. For him, saying sorry to his neglected family was important, but there was also positive action that demonstrated that repentance, in the reordering of his priorities. Again, we shall look at some of these principles later.

I notice with interest that the thing that the Ephesians are to repent of is their lovelessness. Jesus doesn't talk about 'falling out of love', but rather: 'forsaking their first love'. When everyone else was wondering around our wedding reception kissing the beautiful bride and wishing us good luck, one lady whispered in my ear, 'Work hard at it'! It seemed strange at the time, but I am sure it was good advice.

Revive or be Removed!

You need to work hard to keep the fires of your heart warm with affection for God. This involves thinking about his character and love. It involves thinking about the things that first drew you to him.

There are many practical exercises in this book. However, I do not apologize for the fact that there is also quite a bit of 'theology'. This is a scary word. However, all it means is 'knowledge of God'. In other words, if God made marriage, if God uses marriage as an example of his relationship with his people, and if he expects it to be swallowed up in some bigger eternal purpose, then we need to know *God* better in order to revive our marriages!

The challenge of this passage for the Ephesian church is plain. Either their cold heart is warmed up and their hard heart is softened, or their light is removed. Of course, Jesus will continue to shine, but in a loveless, dead church, his witness will be removed. He'll knock their lights out! I am sorry to say that is precisely what happened in Ephesus. There is nothing more than a pile of ruins there now. But there is a promise to the conquerors – overcomers – that they will be allowed to eat from the tree of life again! (Gen 37; cf. 3:22, and Rev. 22:14-15).

Things can easily slip in our relationship with God. Similarly, things can easily slip in our relationships with one another.

John Piper issues a word of warning. If I do not feel joy in life and ministry, then I should not continue, stoically, but rather I should repent:

> [Do not simply] get on with your duty because feelings are irrelevant! My answer has three steps. First, confess the sin of joylessness. Acknowledge the culpable coldness of your heart … Second, pray earnestly that God would restore the joy of obedience. Third, go ahead and do the outward dimension of your duty in the hope that the doing will rekindle the delight.[11]

In the next chapter we shall look at the biblical foundation for a view of marriage which keeps love alive. There is a consistent theme running through the Bible, namely, that God wants intimacy with his people, and that he knows we will be most satisfied in him when we foster that. Marriage is regularly used as an illustration of that intimate relationship, it is a living, breathing, enactment or parable of this kind of love. As we examine the creation accounts of man and woman, we shall look back and remember the height from which we have fallen! Then we shall look forward, beyond God's redemptive work to the final consummation, where we shall enjoy the intimacy with God which the best marriages anticipate.

Fairy Story or Bible Story

The children's film *Shrek* is a wonderful satire on the traditional fairy tale. Once upon a time, there was a terrifying ogre called Shrek. He enjoyed his own company in a dismal swamp. He is furious when his land is invaded by fairly tale characters, escaping the beastly Lord Farquaard. He is joined by the irritating, but eventually loveable, donkey played by Eddie Murphy.

He treks off to confront Lord Farquaard. But before Lord Farquaard will get rid of the unwanted visitors to his swamp, Shrek has to go and rescue Princess Fiona (played by Cameron Diaz) from the dragon-protected fortress, and try to persuade her to marry Lord Farquaard.

Of course, along the way, Shrek falls in love with the princess, and, in fact they do live happily ever after! Then, in *Shrek 2*, the comic fairy tale continues!

Many people's view of marriage is shaped by Hollywood, rather than by the Bible. Fairy tale weddings often don't end up 'happily ever after'.

The Bible account of marriage begins, not with the words 'Once upon a time' but with the words, 'In the beginning, God' (Gen. 1:1). This is no fairy tale, and the happiness promised is not in a romantic, idealistic view of human nature, but rather, in an appreciation that the God who made us, also knows what is best for us.

When making a film or animation, the narrative is usually depicted, scene by scene, on a storyboard. The storyboard gives the main theme of the film and helps the producer and actors get a feel for the overall sequence of the whole film. What would the storyboard look like if we were to make a film about the biblical story of marriage?

Scene 1 – Made in God's Image (Gen. 1:26–28)

Genesis 1:26–28

26 Then God said, 'Let us make man in our image, in our likeness, and let them rule over the fish of the sea and the birds of the air, over the livestock, over all the earth, and over all the creatures that move along the ground.'

27 So God created man in his own image, in the image of God he created him; male and female he created them.

28 God blessed them and said to them, 'Be fruitful and increase in number; fill the earth and subdue it. Rule over the fish of the sea and the birds of the air and over every living creature that moves on the ground.'

As admiring friends coo into the buggy of a newborn baby, they are often heard to say, 'Isn't he like his father?'

The climax to the creation account reminds us that only human beings *image* God. You get a glimpse of what God is like by looking at the hills, the stars, the plant life, or the animal kingdom. But, you see much more of what God is like when you look in the mirror. In human beings, you see a reflection of something of God's own character.

The Image Implies Fruitfulness

In the Ancient Near East, vassal kings would multiply small clay images of themselves and place them at strategic points all across the land. By multiplying images of himself, people were to remember who he is and the vastness of his kingdom. Humans are encouraged to make more images of God, not by removing the rib from the husband's side, but through procreation.

The Image Involves Dominion

The vassal king had another purpose in multiplying his image throughout the land. It served to remind people that wherever they saw his image, there he reigned. So too, human beings show something of God's reign in the way they image him. Men and women do this by creatively ruling the creation.[12]

We shall need to spend some time considering what being 'made in God's image' has to do with living out our married life today.

Genesis 2:22-25

22 Then the LORD God made a woman from the rib he had taken out of the man, and he brought her to the man.

23 The man said, 'This is now bone of my bones and flesh of my flesh; she shall be called 'woman', for she was taken out of man.'

24 For this reason a man will leave his father and mother and be united to his wife, and they will become one flesh.

25 The man and his wife were both naked, and they felt no shame.

Scene 2 – Made Especially for Each Other (Gen. 2:23-25)

Notice the effort which God went to make woman. She was not formed from the dust of the earth, rather, Eve – the handmaid – was hand made! People sometimes say of a young couple who are evidently in love: 'Aren't they made for each other?' There is more than one level to interpret that truth! What more do we learn about the married relationship of the first couple in these verses?

Marriage is for Intimacy

There was no suitable companion for Adam in the rest of creation. But, in Eve, Adam found the answer to loneliness, and a genuine partnership in the work God had given Adam to do in the garden. He exclaimed: 'at last, bone of my bone, flesh of my flesh'. The language used implies a wonderful intimacy. Matthew Henry poetically comments:

> Not made out of his head to top him;
> Nor out of his feet to be trampled upon by him;
> But out of his side to be equal with him,
> under his arm to be protected,
> and near his heart to be loved.[13]

Marriage is for Offspring

Consider these two statements: 'Love-making is the recreation of the species'. 'Love-making is the re-creation of the species'. Both are true.

God could have said, 'Now you're not going to like this, but in order for the human race to continue, you must engage in sexual intercourse!' However, God chose to make love-making one of the most pleasurable of human experiences, celebrated in other parts of the Bible, such as Song of Songs, and intended to be enjoyed in the context of the relationship for which he has designed it.

Marriage is Forever

The phrase, 'one flesh' literally means 'stuck', implying that in marriage, you are 'stuck with each other'! However the Bible means that in a positive sense. Yes, there are circumstances when this glue can be dissolved, but that is not the created intention of the glue! We will see more about the implications of 'one flesh' language later.

<u>Genesis 3:1-8</u>

1 Now the serpent was more crafty than any of the wild animals the LORD God had made. He said to the woman, 'Did God really say, 'You must not eat from any tree in the garden'?'

2 The woman said to the serpent, 'We may eat fruit from the trees in the garden,

3 but God did say, 'You must not eat fruit from the tree that is in the middle of the garden, and you must not touch it, or you will die.''

4 'You will not surely die,' the serpent said to the woman.

5 'For God knows that when you eat of it your eyes will be opened, and you will be like God, knowing good and evil.'

6 When the woman saw that the fruit of the tree was good for food and pleasing to the eye, and also desirable for gaining wisdom, she took some and ate it. She also gave some to her husband, who was with her, and he ate it.

7 Then the eyes of both of them were opened, and they realised that they were naked; so they sewed fig leaves together and made coverings for themselves.

8 Then the man and his wife heard the sound of the LORD God as he was walking in the garden in the cool of the day, and they hid from the LORD God among the trees of the garden.

Scene 3 – God's Good Creation is Spoiled by Sin (Gen. 3)

In Genesis 1–2 everything in the garden is rosy. Even today there is a longing in the human heart to 'go back to Eden'. In Genesis 4 we are shown a picture of the world as we know it, full of anger, jealousy, mistrust, murder. How did we get there? The answer is found in Genesis 3.

Adam and Eve Fall for Satan's Lie (vv. 1–7)

Satan attacks on two fronts. He encourages Adam and Eve to doubt God's word, implying that God is nothing more than a killjoy (vv. 1–2). Further, he encourages them to doubt God's Goodness (vv. 5–6).

Adam and Eve were given the freedom to love God and enjoy open communication with him. Love cannot be coerced. There had to be some test to that love (theologians call it 'probation'). But they failed the test.

Genesis 3:9-23

9 But the LORD God called to the man, 'Where are you?'

10 He answered, 'I heard you in the garden, and I was afraid because I was naked; so I hid.'

11 And he said, 'Who told you that you were naked? Have you eaten from the tree from which I commanded you not to eat?'

12 The man said, 'The woman you put here with me—she gave me some fruit from the tree, and I ate it.'

13 Then the LORD God said to the woman, 'What is this you have done?' The woman said, 'The serpent deceived me, and I ate.'

14 So the LORD God said to the serpent, 'Because you have done this, 'Cursed are you above all the livestock and all the wild animals! You will crawl on your belly and you will eat dust all the days of your life.

15 And I will put enmity between you and the woman, and between your offspring and hers; he will crush your head, and you will strike his heel.'

16 To the woman he said, 'I will greatly increase your pains in childbearing; with pain you will give birth to children. Your desire will be for your husband, and he will rule over you.'

17 To Adam he said, 'Because you listened to your wife and ate from the tree

about which I commanded you, 'You must not eat of it,' 'Cursed is the ground because of you; through painful toil you will eat of it all the days of your life.

18 It will produce thorns and thistles for you, and you will eat the plants of the field.

19 By the sweat of your brow you will eat your food until you return to the ground, since from it you were taken; for dust you are and to dust you will return.'

20 Adam named his wife Eve, because she would become the mother of all the living.

21 The LORD God made garments of skin for Adam and his wife and clothed them.

22 And the LORD God said, 'The man has now become like one of us, knowing good and evil. He must not be allowed to reach out his hand and take also from the tree of life and eat, and live for ever.'

23 So the LORD God banished him from the Garden of Eden to work the ground from which he had been taken.

The Consequences of Sin (vv. 8ff.)

When they heard God walking in the garden, they hid from his presence. What a contrast to the naked, unblushing intimacy of chapter 2! They were ashamed in his presence; thinking they could hide from God. Then they tried to knock him off the scent (v. 10). Finally, they blame each other (vv. 12ff.). Adam said, 'The women you gave me…' Eve responded, 'The serpent deceived me'. As the old joke goes: 'Adam blamed Eve, Eve blamed the serpent, and the serpent didn't have a leg to stand on!'

There is a constant tendency in human relationships, particularly in the so-called 'battle of the sexes', for each to blame the opposite gender for all relationship ills. And there is a failure to square up to the sin which self-evidently is in everyone's life.

The Spoiling Effect of Sin (vv. 14ff.)

The serpent is cursed by God (vv. 14ff.) and ultimately will be crushed. The woman will experience pain in childbirth (v. 16) and the loving complementarity of Genesis 2:23ff. will turn into tyranny and rule. The woman will continue to desire her husband but, rather than giving the godly lead she wants, he exercises dominion over her.

The curse on the man (vv. 17ff.) turns work (a good thing) into toil. This is something we experience in our love/hate relationship with work.

The intimacy the couple once enjoyed with God, and with each other is, for now, lost (v. 24). This is not the end of the story, of course, and even in Genesis there are several indications of God's mercy and grace – he calls them, he promises to crush Satan, and he clothes them – but for now we need to move on in our grand Bible Story.

Scene 4 – God, the Bridegroom; His People, the Bride

There are several Old Testament references (for example, Proverbs 2:16ff.; Isaiah 62:5; Jeremiah 7:34; Ezekiel 16:8; Song of Songs; Malachi 2:14) which include an extended marriage allegory. In this picture/parable, God is likened to the longsuffering bridegroom, initiating and sustaining a covenant relationship. His lovely, but often wayward, bride is the people of Israel. The poetic book Song of Songs has evoked many differences of opinion among biblical scholars as to how much the allegory speaks of the human love between couples, and how much it refers to God's covenant relationship with his people. Whatever the answer to these questions, it is clear that the love and delight which the couple experience points to God's tender, wooing love, towards his people. Only God shows the kind of everlasting love to which Song of Songs points. And, God shows the exclusive covenant jealousy spoken of in the first two commandments (8:6–7).

Scene 5 – Idolatry as Spiritual Adultery

The book of Hosea is the account of a man called Hosea who marries a wayward woman called Gomer. Gomer commits adultery and conceives illegitimate children. Hosea finds her and redeems her from slavery. Gomer said that she loved Hosea, but she ended up breaking Hosea's heart, again and again.

In a similar way, God showed unstinting love towards Israel (chapter 11), but they returned it with immorality and idolatry, leading to God judging them (chapters 12–13). Interweaved throughout this story is the account of Israel's flirtatious relationships with the gods of this world, and God's consistent love.

Like Hosea, God sought to woo back his wayward bride (chapter 14). Throughout the whole account of Hosea, we marvel at the constant show of steadfast, covenant love, a love which takes wayward Israel back. Despite their great rebellion, God shows his amazing commitment to this marriage.

Scene 6 – Christ is the Bridegroom and the Church is the Bride

In the New Testament there are several illustrations of the kind of intimate relationship which Christ has with his people. The most famous parable illustrating the marriage relationship is that of the ten virgins waiting for the return of the bridegroom (although not all commentators agree that the bridegroom here is Christ).

More clear, though, is John the Baptist's description of

Jesus in John 3:22–36. John makes the point that he is just like the best man, helping the groom get ready for his big day. But when the day arrives, the best man fades into the background so that the groom can come and take his bride.

One final illustration in this section, is the famous Ephesians 5:22ff. passage (which we shall look at in more detail later). For now we will restrict our comments to the way in which the marriage relationship is worked out in Christ's relationship with the church, as spoken of in Ephesians 5:31–32:

> 'For this reason a man will leave his father and mother and be united to his wife, and the two will become one flesh.' This is a profound mystery – but I am talking about Christ and the church.

There has been a lot of discussion about the meaning of Paul's phrase 'profound mystery'. The Roman Catholic Church takes this to refer to a sacramental view of marriage. However, this explanation does not help make sense of why Paul takes Genesis 2:24 to refer to Christ and the church, not the human institution of marriage.

Others think that the mystery refers to the union of Christ and the church. In other words, the prime focus of the whole passage is not human marriage, but the allegorical relationship between Christ and the church. However, is there nothing in Ephesians 5:22ff. to learn about human marital relationships?

Better, I think, is to understand 'mystery' as referring to human marriage as a kind of parable of the relationship between Christ and the church. The 'mystery' Paul alludes to would then refer to the 'deeper meaning' of Genesis 2:24, namely, that beyond human marriage, there is a marvellous picture of the divine marriage between Christ and his people.

Clearly this has a lot of implications for Christian marriage which we shall come to later.

What can already be deduced, though, is that to get a full biblical picture of marriage it will involve the 'looking back' and 'looking forward' we referred to in the section on the church in Ephesus, in the last chapter. We need to look back to God's created intention (Gen. 1 and 2); we also need to look forward to the completion of God's work in heaven (the book of Revelation).

To complete our brief Bible survey, let us look at the last few chapters of the Bible story, the book of Revelation.

Scene 7 – The Climax of God's Saving Work will be the Marriage Feast of the Lamb

When quizzed by the Sadducees about the married state of those who are in heaven, Jesus replied, 'At the resurrection people will neither marry nor be given in marriage; they will be like the angels in heaven' (Matt. 22:30). Clearly, in Jesus' mind, there is something temporary about marriage – it is only 'until death do us part'.

In Revelation 19, the scene is one of great rejoicing, because at last, there will be the marriage ceremony between Christ (the lamb) and the bride (the church – see v. 7). We eagerly anticipate the day when God's work among his people will be completed (22:17), and both the church as we know it, and marriage as we know it, will be swallowed up in the creation of the new heaven and the new earth (see Revelation 21).

The Diamond Marriage Course

Our focus here has been the Bible Tale about Marriage, not the Fairy Tale Marriage. Clearly, from this brief survey of what the Bible teaches about the subject, we can see that marriage matters very much to God. Marriage is not just the stuff of fairly tales. Marriage is a human enterprise, which God presides over, and through which God gives eloquent testimony to the world of his eternal purposes! Indeed, as the Church of England Book of Common Prayer advises, not only is the marriage service something which is conducted in the sight of God, but,

> [it] is not by any to be enterprised, nor taken in hand, unadvisedly, lightly, or wantonly, to satisfy men's carnal lusts and appetites, like brute beasts that have no understanding, but reverently, discreetly advisedly, soberly and in the fear of God duly considering the causes for which Matrimony was ordained.

According to the Prayer Book, marriage is ordained by God, for the procreation of children, for a remedy against sin and for the mutual help and comfort of the partners.[14] One should assume, in the light of this brief survey, that Christian couples have a responsibility to foster such a marriage relationship which will give a living picture of the kind of relationship which Christ has fostered with his bride, the church.

It is because I believe that this is a very important theme in the Bible that I have developed a course to help Christian couples live by these principles. The course is called 'The Diamond Marriage', and will be outlined in the rest of this book.

Husband ———————— Wife

Figure 1

Horizontal Implications

The purpose of the sixweek course is to enable Christian couples to develop an understanding of marriage which appreciates both its created intention, and which fosters and maintains joy. Initially, I have discovered, many couples look upon their marriage purely in terms of a 'horizontal' relationship, as illustrated in Figure 1.

Vertical Implications

However, as we shall come to see, there are a number of biblical passages which encourage us to perceive marriage as a triangle, with the Lord as the inextricable third party to a healthy Christian marriage. This is illustrated by the triangle in Figure 2.

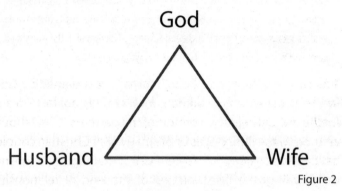

Figure 2

Eternal Implications

Ultimately, however, we will see that the complete biblical picture of marriage is not a triangle, but rather a diamond. This is illustrated by Figure 3(see overleaf). This diagram illustrates the fact that marriage is to be viewed, not just horizontally and vertically, but also, eternally. By understanding more of the eternal purpose of marriage, couples should be able to use their marriage to relate to the world as God intended.

It is my hope that we shall move towards an appreciation of Christian marriage as a diamond. The diamond marriage is one where husband, wife, the Lord and the witness of the marriage to the world, are held together in order to show

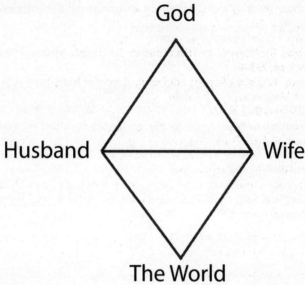

Figure 3

God's ultimate purpose to unite all things in the glorification of his Son.

If this perspective on marriage is grasped, I believe that it will help a couple arrive at their diamond wedding, not only still married – but joyful! This is no fairy tale.

And so we turn to the details of the story…

---

[1] The figures referred to are taken from the Barna Group website (www.barna. org,), research carried out in America. Overall, 33 percent of all born again individuals who have been married have gone through a divorce, which is statistically identical to the 34 percent incidence among non-born again adults.

[2] J. Piper, *Desiring God*, Leicester: IVP, 1986, pp. 1ff.

[3] J. Piper, *The Pleasures of God*, Portland: Multnomah Press, 1991.

[4] Piper, *Desiring God*, pp. 398–9.

[5] C. S. Lewis, *Reflections on the Psalms* Glasgow: Fount Paperbacks, 1987, pp. 80–1.

[6] C. S. Lewis, *The Weight of Glory and Other Addresses*, New York: Harper Collins, 2000, p. 26.

[7] http://www.ravenhill.org/edwards.htm

[8] J. Edwards, *The Works of Jonathan Edwards*, Edinburgh: Banner of Truth, 1998, vol. I, pp. 753–9.

[9] J. Edwards, *Religious Affections*, Edinburgh: Banner of Truth, 1994, p. 27.

[10] Edwards, *Religious Affections*, p. 46.

[11] Piper, *Desiring God*, p. 221.

[12] I am indebted to Richard Pratt for this insight. See *Designed for Dignity*, Phillipsburg: P and R Publishing, 1993

[13] M. Henry, *A Commentary on the Whole Bible:,Genesis–Deuteronomy*, Iowa Falls: Word Bible Publishers (no date), vol. 1, p.20

[14] The Alternative Service Book and Common Worship place companionship higher up the priority list than procreation, which is interesting, but not our main point here.

PART 1

BUILDING THE

HORIZONTAL RELATIONSHIP

BETWEEN HUSBAND AND WIFE

1

Biblical Perspectives On The Relationship

It was the night before their wedding day and the young couple were having a final rehearsal with the clergyman. The bride was particularly concerned that she would not be able to remember what to say or where to go on her big day!

Eventually, the minister said to her, 'Look, it really is quite a simple ceremony. I will meet you at the bottom of the aisle and you walk up to stand next to your husband before the altar. You exchange vows to each other and then we have a final hymn. It really couldn't be easier. If you remember this, then everything will be fine tomorrow.'

This seemed to placate the nervous bride. However, the following day the congregation were shocked to hear the young lady muttering under her breath as she walked towards her fiancé: 'Aisle, altar, hymn; aisle, altar, hymn.'

Of course, to begin a marriage assuming that you can change your spouse's irritating habits or personality defects is a recipe for disaster. In our normal course of life, we assume that the way things are now is the way they have always been. But this is not the case. The way things are now, is in continuity with the way things have always been, but it is also true that things are different to how they used to be.

Our common experiences as Christians include an awareness of the wonder of God's goodness in creation, as well as an appreciation of the pervasive effect of the fall.[1]

Bearing this in mind, I want to steer a path between an idealism – which paints an unrealistic and unattainable view of marriage (the fairy tale marriage); and a fatalism – which assumes that bad marriages cannot be restored and good marriages cannot be made (many people's experience of marriage). Biblical marriage, on the other hand, is neither idealistic, nor is it assumed that, even despite the fall, it is unattainable.

In order to achieve this, we do need to look at the way God intended things to be. I am in good company, here, actually. Jesus and the apostle Paul both cite Genesis 2:24 as the foundational text on biblical marriage. When the Pharisees quiz Jesus about his attitude to divorce he seems reluctant to be drawn into the debate. He responds to their questions by reminding them that God's created design is that marriage should be for life. It is not part of the creator's intention that marriages should be dissolved (see Matt. 19:5; Mark 10:8).In effect, Jesus seems to be saying, 'Don't begin your argument from the perspective of your common experience, rather, go back to God's original plan'.

The apostle Paul also cites this text to lay his foundational teaching on Christian marriage (see Eph. 5:32). While Jesus quoted this text to Jewish Pharisees, steeped in the Old Testament text, Paul seems to primarily have a Gentile audience in mind when he writes. Their comments were addressed to very different religious, cultural and social settings, but they assumed that this text was a fundamental, universal understanding of marriage.

So, we too must begin here. However, by way of an aside, I want to pick up on the question of divorce. This is not my primary subject here, but I appreciate that *most* people are not beginning their marriage from the perspective of the 'created ideal'. Rather, we all begin from the post-Genesis perspective of sin and failure, which for some means fornication, adultery or divorce.[2] I will have a little more to say about dealing with the 'baggage' which we each bring to our marriage in later chapters.

However, we should notice the way in which the New Testament writers speak about marriage. There seems to be an acknowledgment of the seriousness of the issue of divorce, and a realism about its effect, while not allowing it to detract from the ideal for which we are created.

One helpful analogy might be to think about 'Super Glue'. When this product first came on the market there was considerable concern about the impact of making, readily available, such a strong adhesive. People discovered that, if they were not careful, not only did they use the glue to join two things together, but they also sometimes found themselves joined to other things by mistake – the lid of the glue, or the table or perhaps other parts of their body! Hence, in order to deal with this problem, the manufacturers supplied an additional smaller bottle with the tube of glue to be used to dissolve any inadvertent joinings. No one was under any illusion that glue was not intended to stick. However it was recognized that in certain circumstances such a dissolution was necessary and desirable.

Like most analogies, this one is imperfect. However, it does help remind us that the created intention for marriage is to join man and woman together in a one-flesh, indissoluble union. At the same time, the Bible appears to proscribe certain circumstances in which the marriage may be dissolved.

My point here is not so much to argue for the circumstances in which these dissolutions may occur.[3]

My point, rather, is to say that it is not part of the created intention of the marriage bond to be dissolved, even though God himself seems to proscribe circumstances where the dissolution may happen.

Genesis 2:24, therefore, is the place where we must begin, for we must understand the nature of the marriage bond. The Old Testament writer, Gerhard von Rad comments on the place of this verse in the context of the passage:

> A fact needs explanation, namely, the extremely powerful drive of the sexes to each other. Whence comes this love 'strong as death' (Song of Songs 8:6) and stronger than the tie to one's own parents... this drive towards each other which does not rest until it again becomes one flesh in the child?[4]

When God initiated the first ever marriage, the occasion was marked by great joy. If I may paraphrase Adam's reaction, he exclaims, 'At last! Here she is!' (Gen. 2:23). The answer to man's loneliness was not found in the whole of the rest creation. So God *handmade* Eve (his *handmaid!*), and when Adam sees her he is very excited, 'Woah, Man!' he exclaims, and so she is named Woman. Well, that's not quite a literal translation, but it gets to the heart of the joy which Adam experienced when he first saw his new wife. We shall spend some time looking at these verses, but the sheer fact that 2:24 is quoted so much in the rest of the Bible gives us an indication of how foundational this perspective on marriage is to understanding and living by it today.

There has been a lot of scholarly writing about the difference between the creation accounts recorded in Genesis 1 and 2. Much of this discussion is quite obscure and technical. However, one question does require an answer: What is the reason for the differences between the creation accounts of the man and the woman? For, this question is relevant to our understanding of Christian marriage.

At the end of Genesis 1, man is presented as the climax of God's creation (see 1:26). He alone is made in the image of God (this refers to both the male and the female, see 1:27). God saw all that he had made and 'it was very good' (1:31).

In chapter 2 we come across something that 'is not good', namely, that the man should be alone. Hence (vv. 18–22) the writer explains the creation of Eve as the answer to man's loneliness. This is an extraordinary act of creation, where God is literally 'hands on', not making her by word alone.

There are a number of unique features about the creation of Eve which hint at the kind of role she and Adam are to play. First, God took the women from the man – they were originally one flesh. Second, she is made differently, from Adam's rib, not from the dust of the earth. Third, Adam is absolutely delighted when he sees her: 'Bone of my bone, flesh of my flesh,' he exclaims! He is filled with joy at the sight of Eve and bursts into song!

We can deduce from this that there is something about Eve which makes him complete, she is his creative counterpart and can meet his loneliness in a way that none of the animals of the garden were able. Remember Matthew Henry's delightful comment?

> Not made out of his head to top him, not out of his feet to be trampled upon by him, but out of his side to be equal with him, under his arm to be protected, and near his heart to be loved.[5]

Here is the first marriage service! God, like the father of the bride, presents his beautiful daughter to Adam. God also acts as officiating minister, with Moses commenting, that those whom God has joined together, no man should separate:

'For this reason a man will leave his father and mother and be united to his wife, and they will become one flesh' (Gen. 2:24).

In a very real sense, then, marriage is not a mere social convenience, or even just a religious ceremony. Rather it is to be seen as a reuniting of the man and the women at the deepest level of their creation, as real as if the bone and flesh were joined together to make one new person again!

There are a number of practical implications which flow from these verses in Genesis 2. First, we note that both the bride and bridegroom are to leave their own families and be brought into a new unity. From two distinct and separate families, one new family unit is formed. Second, the marriage is to be exclusive (leaving one family to form another); it is to be permanent (implied by the words 'cleave' or 'be united'), and it is to involve the formation of a new family unit ('one flesh'). Third, marriage is not merely a private arrangement, rather, the personal relationship between two people is brought into a public social ceremony. But this public ceremony is to be matched by a private consummation and ongoing union.

Let us look at each of these three stages:

- **'Leaving'** involves an emotional as well as a physical separation from one's parents. Many of the marriage problems I come across have to do with the failure to properly 'leave home'. Maybe the wife runs home to Mum whenever there is tension at home. Or perhaps the husband shows overdependence on his mother. The Bible has a lot to say about the responsibility we all have towards our parents (not least, the fourth commandment). But this passage implies that after marriage we have a greater responsibility of loyalty to our spouse over our parents.

- **'Cleaving'** implies forsaking all others and sticking to an exclusive relationship. It is language which the Bible writers will use to describe the exclusive relationship Israel must have with the Lord, by forsaking other gods (see Deut. 10:20; 11:22; 13:5). We saw earlier that many people have seen this kind of covenant language applied to the marriage relationship as well. David Atkinson believes that the covenant language includes four main areas: faithfulness to a vow, faithfulness to a calling, faithfulness to a person, faithfulness to a relationship.[6]

These four areas of the covenant relationship have much to say about the way in which the husband and wife are to 'cleave' to each other. It includes the need to 'mean what we say' in the wedding vows which we made. It also includes the idea that we must stick close by, and love with loyalty, the person whom we have married.

- **'One flesh'** involves, first, an intention, and second, a growing experience. To be 'one flesh' implies more than just sexual intercourse, although that can clearly be inferred. The force of the word is more to do with a social than a sexual union. It is the process of becoming 'one'. At one level this happens as soon as the couple are married, but at a deeper level, the couple increasingly experience 'being one'. 'Bone of my bones and flesh of my flesh' was how Adam described it. We sometimes joke about how a person and her dog seem to look alike! But there is a very real sense in which the husband and wife increasingly *do* become alike.

There may be some truth in the assertion that 'opposites attract', and certainly God intended marriage to be more than the cloning of two identical characters, for the whole force of the 'complementary relationship' is such that they 'fit together' – socially, physically and spiritually. If this is the case, then the couple's inseparable marriage bond will also result in a mixing and a merging of two personalities into one flesh. Couples on the marriage course I run all talk of their similarities being an important glue in their relationship which enables them better to celebrate their diversity.

Before their sin evicted them from the garden, the writer comments on Adam and Eve's unashamed and unhindered intimacy (Gen. 2:25). Here was a relationship with absolute openness and honesty.

Have you seen the film *Under the Tuscan Sun* (2004)? The story is very simple. Diane Lane plays a recently divorced, middle-aged San Francisco writer. The divorce has been painful and made her feel isolated and directionless in life. Her friends try to persuade her that she needs to get out of the country with them, for a ten-day holiday in Tuscany. Initially, she is very hesitant, but they eventually persuade her to go, and she ends up falling in love with Tuscany and impulsively buying and renovating a dilapidated house. It is well worth watching!

One line in the film caught my attention. I was interested in the reason why she was so reluctant to move on with her life after her divorce. She initially responds to her friends' invitation to go to Italy by saying, 'Why don't you die after you get divorced? It feels like you should. Is it not supposed to be "till death do us part"?'

These are interesting sentiments which get to the heart of what it means to be 'one flesh' and why this union is intended to be indissoluble until death. By merging two persons into one flesh, it is not intended they can be easily unscrambled without pain and loss.

Summary

What have we seen so far about the marriage relationship as spelled out in Genesis?

First, Genesis 1 teaches that both the man and the woman are made in God's image. In their marriage they will find fulfilment and intimacy with a co-equal partner. There is no room for superiority or domineering here.

Second, God had a very 'hands on' approach to creating Eve. No animal was able to fulfil the role for which Eve was made. She was specially created from a part of Adam, his own flesh. Adam names her. The Genesis narrative intends us to deduce Adam's role as including a degree of initiating and leading in the relationship, with her responding and yielding to him.

Third, the first marriage ceremony was one of great joy and delight! Finally, Adam is happy. The woman is 'bone of my bones and flesh of my flesh', he says (Gen. 2:23), and in her, he will find contentment and companionship in the task of looking after the world in which God has placed them.

In the next chapter we will work out some of the practical implications of these key verses. A right understanding of Genesis 2:24 leads us to conclude that healthy, and thereby joy-filled, marriages require the couple to understand and live out their individual roles within the marriage and also work out their corporate roles together. This text needs to be combined with Genesis 1:27–28 in order to gain a complete picture of the individual and corporate roles both marriage partners play in the marriage.

By their 'individual roles' I mean that each partner in the marriage has distinct but complementary roles to play. I take the term 'corporate roles' to imply that there are ways in which the couple, now 'one flesh', act jointly as if one singular person. This corporate role has implications for their relationship with God and in the society in which they live. More on this later.

When I teach the Diamond Marriage Course, I have two main audiences in mind. With engaged couples and newly weds (those in the first three years of marriage) I emphasize the fact that God has created marriage in order that something of his eternal purposes might be revealed in the human relationship we know as marriage. Once this perspective on marriage is appreciated, our homes and families can be better used to testify to God's bigger purposes. We need a sense of purpose in anything that we do if we are going to maintain our joy. This is no less true for marriage.

When teaching older couples, I spend some time emphasizing that joylessness in marriage is not something to be acquiesced in, but rather, it is something to be repented of and replaced with true joy. There are a number of practical ways in which we can revive our joy and, even if you have been married for a long time, it is possible that 'the first love' (and joy) of which Revelation speaks, may be yours again!

Joy in the Bible

We have noted already that 'joy' is not something that is an added extra in the Christian life. Rather, joy is essential to a healthy Christian life. The passage we have just looked at in Genesis 2 concludes that Adam found absolute joy in his wife. This is integral to the health of that marriage.

With these things in mind, it is worth spending a few moments looking at the key biblical passages which speak about Christian joy:

Joy is Not Optional

The authors of the Westminster Shorter Catechism were clear about the role of joy in the Christian life, for the answer to the first question, 'What is the chief end of man?' is: 'The chief end of man is to glorify God and enjoy him forever'. The Bible argues that we are made for a joyful relationship with God, but sin separates us from him and spoils the good things he has made, leading to, among other things, loss of joy (John 3:16–21; Rom. 1:18–2:16; Rev. 22:11–15).

Human beings react very differently to life's diverse circumstances, of course. Our experiential and emotional reactions are uniquely individual and we should neither despise them nor allow them to be our master. These two statements are no less true when it comes to talking about Christian marriage. Later we will consider some of the biblical teaching about our complementary differences which mean that men and women respond to marriage issues rather differently. But for the moment I want to establish that joy is assumed to be the normal part of normal Christianity!

Joy is not the same things as jollity. Temperamentally, each person is different. A melancholic Christian may experience Christian joy and an extravert non-Christian may not.

John Piper's life mission statement, adopted by Bethlehem Baptist Church in Minneapolis, is 'God is most glorified in us when we are most satisfied in him'. Piper pleads for a pervasive God-centredness in all of life and worship. He contends that our satisfaction, pleasure and delight is not ultimately at odds with God's design for us. God not only wants us to be holy, but also to be happy.

'Christianity isn't a Joy ride, but a Joy Road'

In the book from which I have just quoted, *Laid Back Christianity*, Dr J. I. Packer makes some pertinent comments about Christian teaching on joy, from which I make the following observations:[7]

- Joy is being able to experience the gravity of some of life's circumstances and the reality of our human and spiritual position, and at the same time having joy (2 Cor. 6:10).

- Joy is commanded by the apostle Paul, which implies that it is more than a whooshy feeling (Phil. 1:4; 1:18; 2:2; 3:1; 4:4).

- Joy is one of the hallmarks of authentic Christian experience (Rom. 14:17; Gal. 5:22).

- Joy is not fully experienced in this life – it is, but an anticipation of heaven. Amazingly, it is the thought of martyrdom which brings about joy, for the apostle Paul (Phil. 1:19–26). This was Jesus' joy too (Heb. 12:2). Joy is anticipated now, as a foretaste of heaven, and because the joy of heaven will be so great we may experience joy even when the road is very bumpy, for we know joy is not deferred forever. Even on the night before his death, with the certainty of the cross ahead for Jesus and desertion and ultimately persecution for his followers, Jesus told the disciples that joy could be complete if they kept in obedience to his love (John 15:11).

Where Does Christian Joy Come From?

If joy is an integral part of healthy marriages, and that joy is tied up with a healthy individual and corporate Godward focus, then we need to know how joy can be fostered and developed.

1. Joy comes from an appreciation that the believer is accepted in Christ and loved. Indeed we should be awestruck by the amazing love and grace that has been lavished on us by the Father in sending the Son (Rom. 8:32, 38ff.).

2. It has well been said that happiness comes from circumstances, but joy comes from the knowledge of our relationship with the Lord. Consequently even imprisoned and possibly near martyrdom, Paul can instruct believers to rejoice in the Lord always (hence Phil. 4:11ff.). Our joy is found in knowing the truth of Romans 8:28, that generally God does not make us happy by removing our circumstances, but rather he gives us joy in our circumstances, knowing that he is using them to mould us into the image of Jesus. His good purposes spoken of in this verse includes a life of conformity to his will.

3. As I have already mentioned above, joy comes from realizing that we are saved for an eternity with God in whom is fullness of joy forever more.

4. James wrote 'Consider it pure joy, my brothers whenever you face trials of many kinds because you know that the testing of your faith produces perseverance...' Trials are to be received joyfully because we know that through them God is routing out our sinful dispositions and leading us to trust him more.

5. Joy comes from an habitual response to God. Galatians 5:16–26 is an important passage. The fruit of the Spirit is

produced by our crucifying the sinful nature and being led by the Spirit. In other words, the link between a serious attitude towards sin and a life of joy is inextricable. Because sin is our fundamental problem it is only by first saying 'no' that we can say 'yes'. Christian qualities are not things we can cultivate by ourselves. They are not the result of some amazing self-improvement plan. No, rather these characteristics are the overflow of a life abiding in Christ and remaining in him; a life starving the flesh, crucifying it, and a life walking in and by the Holy Spirit.

Summary and Implications

The unity of husband and wife in one flesh means that the couple now relate the principles of Christian hedonism to their corporate relationship:

> The Biblical mandate to husbands and wives is to seek your own joy in the joy of your spouse. Good done to the bride is good done to yourself because you are one flesh.... For a husband to be an obedient person he must love his wife the way Christ loved the Church. That is, he must pursue his own joy in the holy joy of his wife.[8]

You cannot exclude self-interest from love, Piper comments (see more on this below). The problem with marriage is not that we seek happiness; rather 'selfishness seeks its own private happiness at the expense of others. Love seeks its happiness in the happiness of the beloved'.[9]

J. I. Packer notes that the Puritans were the first to revive a much more healthy, biblical view of the role of sex and intimacy within marriage:

> Chrysostom had denied that Adam and Eve could have had sexual relations before the Fall; Augustine allowed that procreation was lawful, but insisted that

the passions accompanying intercourse were always sinful.... Gregory of Nyssa was sure that Adam and Eve had been made without sexual desire, and that had there been no Fall mankind would have produced by means of what Leland Ryken gravely calls 'some harmless mode of vegetation' ... so twisted a record urgently needed to be set straight, and this the Reformers, followed by the Puritans, forthrightly did.[10]

Packer goes on to quote Richard Baxter as typifying the Puritan view that marriage was for mutual pleasure and enjoyment in the sight of God:

I pray you, tell me my duty to my wife and hers to me.

The common duty of husband and wife is,

1. Entirely to love each other; and therefore choose one that is truly lovely... and avoid all things that tend to quench your love.

2. To dwell together and enjoy each other, and faithfully join as helpers in the education of their children, the government of the family, and the management of their worldly business.

3. Especially to be helpers of each other's salvation: to stir up each other to faith, love and obedience, and good works: to warn and help each other against sin, and all temptations; to join in God's worship in the family, and in private: to prepare each other for the approach of death, and comfort each other in the hopes of life eternal.

4. To avoid all dissensions, and to bear with those infirmities in each other which you cannot cure: to assuage, and not provoke, unruly passions; and, in lawful things, to please each other.

5. To keep conjugal chastity and fidelity, and to avoid all unseemly and immodest carriage with another, which may stir up jealousy; and yet to avoid all jealousy which is unjust.

6. To help one another to bear their burdens (and not by impatience to make them greater). In poverty, crosses, sickness, dangers, to comfort and support each other. And to be delightful companions in holy love, and heavenly hopes and duties, when all other outward comforts fail.[11]

The next chapter is the first of three chapters building on the principles which we have looked at so far in this section of the book. The practical exercises are designed to help build and maintain what may be called 'the horizontal access', namely, the primary relationship between the husband and the wife.

The old best man's witticism: 'Marriage isn't a word but a sentence – a long sentence (with no parole)' may get a laugh at the wedding reception, but it is reflective of some people's view too! My point is that the Bible assumes that marriage is not just to be endured, but to be enjoyed. For marriage is part of a God ordained structural relationship, or covenant, between the husband and wife in the sight of God. We need to turn, next, to some of the practical implications of this primary relationship.

---

[1] We shall also need to look at the impact of the redeeming work of Christ in restoring our marriages. This we will do in Chapter 3.

[2] I am using biblical terminology here: 'fornication' refers to sex outside of marriage (premarital sex or sex with someone who you are not married to); 'adultery' refers to sex with someone who is already married, or sex with someone else while you are in a married relationship.

[3] See A. Cornes, *Divorce and Remarriage: Biblical Principles and Pastoral Practice*, Mentor/ Christian Focus, Fearn Ross-shire, 2003 (out of print).

[4] G. von Rad, *Genesis 1-11*, London: SCM Press, 1971.

[5] Henry, *Genesis-Deuteronomy*, vol. 1, p. 20.

[6] D. Atkinson, *The Message of Genesis 1-11*, Leicester: IVP, 1990.

[7] J. I. Packer, *Laid Back Religion*, Leicester: IVP, 1987.

[8] Piper, *Desiring God*, pp. 171-2.

[9] Piper, *Desiring God*, p. 173.

[10] J. I. Packer, *Among God's Giants*, Eastbourne: Kingsway, 1991, p. 343.

[11] J. I. Packer, *Among God's Giants*, pp. 345-6.

2

BUILDING INTIMACY

Married life is very frustrating: in the first year of marriage the man speaks and the wife listens; in the second year the woman speaks and the husband listens; in the third year they both speak and the neighbours listen!

Marriage is a three-ring circus: engagement ring; wedding ring; and suffering!

Part of the reason for such cynical reactions to marriage is the sheer difficulty of merging two personalities into one flesh! When you add to this the multiple roles of husband, father, lover, provider, and wife, housekeeper, mother and lover, to mention but a few, we feel very stretched.

The 1979 film, *Multiplicity*, stars Michael Keaton as Doug Kinney, an overworked family man in desperate need of a holiday. A rather eccentric scientist offers him an enticing solution to his problems: he will make him a clone of himself. Doug is excited to find that his clone will do all his menial work chores! Soon, of course he needs another clone to help with household chores and, before he realizes what he is doing, Doug has four clones of himself. Each of these clones has personality problems and they start to confuse his wife, played by Andie MacDowell, who is unable to account for his seemingly erratic behaviour. It is all good Hollywood fun!

But, the possibility of human cloning seems to be coming a step closer (as reported in the newspapers on 13 February 2004). Scientists in South Korea claim to have created human embryos through cloning and extracted embryonic stem cells, the universal cells that hold great promise for medical research. The ethical problems associated with these actions are enormous, but they are not our prime concern here.

In our last chapter we notice, very obviously, that God didn't make a clone of Adam. He made a complementary partner. God did not choose to duplicate Adam, rather, he instructed Adam and Eve to fill the earth with unique human beings, each made in the image of God, through procreation.

Adam and Eve's relationship is unique. None of the other animals in God's kingdom enjoy such intimacy in an exclusive, unashamed honest relationship. At its best, marriage provides a safe place for a man or a woman to open themselves up honestly to another human being. Even at its most trying, marriage provides an intimacy which is not found in any other human relationship as is illustrated in Winston Churchill's marriage.

Churchill was once at a dinner banquet when the guests were all asked, 'If you were not who you are, who would you most like to be?' His dear wife, Clemmie was seated next to him, and along with her, the curious dinner guests were keen to hear the great man's response. Churchill's wise and diplomatic reply was, 'If I could not be who I am, I would most like to be Lady Churchill's second husband.' What a diplomat![1]

They did have a stormy, but very loyal, relationship. On one occasion his wife, Clementine, wrote to him about his bumptious and overbearing manner. Notice the way she defends him publicly, and yet challenges him privately with honesty and gentleness:

> I hope you'll forgive me if I tell you something that I feel you ought to know. One of the men in your entourage, a devoted friend, has been to me and told me that there is a danger of your being generally disliked by your colleagues and subordinates, because of your rough, sarcastic and overbearing manner. I was astonished and upset, because in all these years I've been accustomed to all those you've worked with, and under you, loving you. I said this, and I was told, 'No doubt it's the strain.' My darling Winston, I must confess that I have noticed a deterioration in your manner, and you're not so kind as you used to be. With this terrific power as Prime Minister, you must combine urbanity, kindness and, if possible, Olympic calm. Besides, you won't get the best results by irascibility and rudeness. Please forgive your loving, devoted, and watchful, Clemmie.[2]

How then do two individual, self-contained human beings merge and marry into a one flesh relationship?

Individual and Corporate Roles in Marriage

> A long marriage is two people trying to dance a duet and two solos at the same time.
>
> Anne Taylor Fleming in
> *Town and Country* magazine

When teaching the Diamond Marriage Course, I aim to show that a right understanding of Genesis 2:24 leads us to conclude that healthy, and thereby joy-filled, marriages require the couple to understand and live out their individual roles within the marriage and also work out their corporate roles together.

By their 'individual roles' I mean that each partner in the marriage has distinct but complementary roles to play. I take the term 'corporate roles' to imply that there are ways in which the couple, now 'one flesh', act jointly as if one singular person. This corporate role has implications for their relationship with God and in the society in which they live.

In each of the following three areas of married life (creation, redemption and heaven) we explore the individual and corporate roles within marriage.

Before we turn to the practical implications of the 'horizontal axis' let me introduce the meat of the Diamond Marriage Course:

Joy in Creation – Horizontal Building

This section involves examining the implications of Genesis 2:24 and its surrounding context in Genesis 1–2 for building joy-filled and healthy marriages.

- Individually – Joy is found in an appreciation of the created distinctiveness between husband and wife.
  Goal: To understand the expression of joy in Genesis 2:24, 'bone of my bones', in a way that will lead the couple to appreciate the richness of their created humanity and foster enjoyment in and through creation.
- Corporately – Joy is found in creation as a corporate experience shared by the husband and wife in God's created world.
  Goal: To understand the implications of Genesis 1:27, namely that the man and woman together jointly image God through multiplication and dominion. When the husband and wife fill the world with further images of God through procreation, and when jointly they exercise dominion over the created world, the couple experience joy in and through all that God has made.

Joy in Redemption – Vertical Building

This section involves exploring the implications of Ephesians 5:21–33. The conclusion of this study will be to encourage the building up of the husband and wife relationship in the sight of, and with the help of, God.

- Individually – Joy is found when each partner first looks after the rights or needs of their beloved.
  Goal: To enable couples to appreciate the Ephesian teaching that when wives submit to their husbands as the church does to Christ, and when husbands love their wives as Christ loved the church, both partners find their needs met and their joy maximized. Such fulfilled relationships will only happen when the husband and wife see Christ the Lord behind the way each partner in the marriage relates to the other.
- Corporately – Joy is maximized jointly when the couple learn to see their marriage as a living illustration of God's saving plans for fallen humanity.
  Goal: To help the husband and wife appreciate that the prime marriage to which Genesis 2:24 applies is Christ and his church, and encourage them to witness to the world of God's redemptive plans by finding joy in their joint relationship, thereby displaying something of God's big plan for marriage.

Joy in Heaven – Eternal Building

This section considers the eternal purposes God has for marriage and examines some of the implications of Paul's application of Genesis 2:24 in Ephesians 5:32.

- Individually – Joy is found when any person realizes that heaven will ultimately answer the human longing for intimacy and companionship.

  Goal: To appreciate that whatever a person's marital state on earth, they will experience true marriage in heaven and, like the angels, enjoy the fullness of experience with God (Matt. 22:29–31).

- Corporately – Fullness of joy will be found in heaven at the marriage of God's bride (the church) to God's Son. In heaven there will be no more death, mourning, crying or pain (Rev. 21:4).

  Goal: To help husbands and wives appreciate that human marriage is penultimate, not ultimate, and thereby live their lives in expectation of the final completion of God's work at Jesus' return.

The purpose of this course is to help Christian couples work towards six key goals for their marriage – corporate and individual goals in each of the three areas: horizontal, vertical and eternal. The end result will be an appreciation of Christian marriage as a diamond. The diamond marriage is one where husband, wife, the Lord and the witness of the marriage to the world, are held together in order to show God's ultimate purposes to unite all things in the glorification of his Son.

Each section begins with a set of preparation questions which are completed by participating couples, in advance of the session. It is helpful if each couple can prepare answers to these questions individually and then discuss them as a couple before each session.[3]

Responses to these questions may be shared at the beginning of the session by way of introduction to the teaching component for the day. The bulk of the evening will involve teaching on the topic for the day, followed by suggested practical exercises designed to earth the teaching in day-to-day married life. Preparation questions for the following week need to be thought through during the week in order that couples may come prepared for the following week's topic.

Let us return, then to the exercises associated with this chapter in which we shall build upon the creation marriage principles we have looked at so far.

Joy in Creation – Practical Exercises to Help Horizontal Building

Preparation Questions

Every marriage begins with high ideals.

- What expectations did you have for your marriage?
- Did you discuss your future marriage together?
- Do you still hold to those principles? How many of those expectations were unrealistic ideals, and how many were good principles which may need reviving?
- To what extent do you think that your marriage has matured?
- To what extent do you think that you have lost some of the good ideals you began with?
- Have you set any recent goals for your marriage? Should you?
- How might an understanding of Genesis 1–2 help you improve your relationship with your spouse?

Practical Exercises

Leave, Cleave, One Flesh

Leave

The word 'leave' could be translated 'abandon' because it refers to a radical departure from one's birth home and family.

- Are there areas in your relationship with your parents and in-laws that may suggest that you have not 'left' home?
- When it comes to deciding a place to live, schooling of the children, structure of your family home or allocation of time, do you put your spouse above your parents' interests?
- Do you work hard at praising one another – particularly in the presence of others?
- Do you have previous or current social or sexual relationships which you need to leave?
- Have you developed a happy and meaningful relationship with your in-laws? How can you be close to them, and offer care for them, without losing the space your marriage needs?

Cleave

'Cleaving' includes the idea of sticking to each other with steadfast loyalty.

- Do you see the husband/wife relationship as primary?
- Have you recognized temperamental/personality differences which impinge upon your relationship together? Have you resolved to improve yourself rather than seek to change your spouse?!
- How can you be sure that you do not substitute children/parents where husband/wife should be?

- Do you make sure that you have time together as a couple? Arrange to go on a date night with your spouse and try to do something they enjoy most.
- Have you recently recalled your marriage vows? Find some time to do this and remind your spouse that you still mean them!

The Bridegroom's Promise	The Bride's Promise
I (_____) take you (_____),	I (_____) take you (_____),
to be my wife,	to be my husband,
to have and to hold	to have and to hold
from this day forward;	from this day forward;
for better, for worse,	for better, for worse,
for richer, for poorer,	for richer, for poorer,
in sickness and in health,	in sickness and in health,
to love, cherish and worship,	to love, cherish and obey,
till death us do part,	till death us do part,
according to God's holy law;	according to God's holy law;
and this is my solemn vow.	and this is my solemn vow.

- Read through Revelation 2:1–7.
- Examine the relationship between Christ and the Ephesian church and consider what is implied about reviving the first love in your relationship:
  - o In what areas do you need to remember your first love (vv. 4–5a)?
  - o Are there things of which you must repent (v. 5b)?
  - o What kind of habits or disciplines might you need to revive (v. 5b)?

One flesh

This phrase speaks of the new body/single unit that the two married people now make. They are united in an indissolvable union.

- *Social Oneness* (1 Cor. 6:16). 'One flesh' principles imply that the husband and wife should become one with each other. This does not mean that they have no separate activities. However, they may need to find things that they can do together as well as separately. Peter encourages husbands to 'live with their wives' (1 Pet. 3:7). Do you merely inhabit the same dwelling? Or do you live joint lives? Do you really know each other?
- *Sexual Oneness*. Being 'one flesh' clearly assumes that there will be physical intimacy between husband and wife. We shall explore this subject in greater detail later.
  - o Reading a book such as *Intended for Pleasure*, can help revive enjoyment in this area of the relationship. Trying some of the following may be helpful.[4]
  - o Have a night in together without the telephone plugged in.
  - o Eat a leisurely meal together.

o Have an evening without the television on, listening to music, talking, or massaging each other…

o Organize someone to look after the children for a night if that is possible, so that you can go away from home for a romantic break.

o Change your routine in lovemaking: time of day, venue and so on.

- *Spiritual Oneness*. Consider the implications of the following passages of scripture: 1 Corinthians 3:16; 6:16-17; 2 Corinthians 6:14; 1 Thessalonians 5:18; Philippians 4:11-13.

o Have you cultivated a spiritual dimension to your marriage relationship?

o When do you find time to read the Bible and pray together?

o Have you thought about the implications for the spiritual union you now enjoy with each other?

o What kind of things do you pray about for your marriage?

o Look again at 1 Corinthians 6:12–20. What is implied about the spiritual oneness which the one flesh relationship brings?

Paradise Lost

Here we address some of the issues which are associated with Genesis 3:

- *Feelings of shame*. It may be that you will have to discover whether these feelings are legitimate and therefore repentance is needed; or whether they are there because of misplaced guilt about former relationships, lack of self-confidence or other failures.

- *Blame-shifting.* Try to break cycles of incrimination when things go wrong. Be quick to apologize and remember the principle of Ephesians 4:26. Resolve to talk through differences in private without sarcasm, aggression or bitterness. Sometimes it may be helpful to do this with a mature married couple or a marriage counsellor.

- *Dissatisfaction in gender roles.* Appreciate the pressure modern society puts upon both the man and the woman. Try to work out domestic chores and who is going to make big decisions about things – such as money, holidays, discipline of children, time off, and how those decisions will be shared out.

Enjoying Creation

Spend time enjoying the richness of God's creation and the diversity of all that he has made. In particular, appreciate the creative talents God has distributed between husband and wife, and enjoy each other's complementary skills and roles. Learn to love your similarities and your differences.

---

[1] J. Humes, *Churchill: Speaker of the Century*, New York: Stein and Day, 1980, p. 291.

[2] *Winston and Clementine: The Personal Letters of The Churchills in USA*, edited by Mary Soames, London and Boston 1999, written on June 27, 1940.

[3] The Course material is available for download, please see Appendix 2 for details

[4] See E. and G. Wheat, *Intended for Pleasure: Sex Technique and Sexual Fulfilment in Christian Marriage*, London: Scripture Union, 1977 or Tim and Beverly LaHaye, *The Act of Marriage: The Beauty of Sexual Love*, Grand Rapids: Zondervan, 1998. See also, N. and S. Lee, *The Marriage Book*, London: HTB Publications, 2000.

PART 2

BUILDING THE

VERTICAL RELATIONSHIP BETWEEN

HUSBAND, WIFE AND GOD

3

THE MARRIAGE TRIANGLE (EPHESIANS 5:21-32)

The Battle of the Sexes

Men and women have consistently joked about one another's differences and perceived weaknesses. Consider some of the following remarks:

"Any husband who says, 'My wife and I are completely equal partners,' is talking about either a law firm or a hand of bridge."

Bill Cosby

"Keep your eyes wide open before marriage, half shut afterwards."

Benjamin Franklin

"My wife dresses to kill. She cooks the same way."

Henry Youngman

"My wife and I were happy for twenty years. Then we met."

Rodney Dangerfield.

"A husband said to his wife, 'No, I don't hate your relatives. In fact, I like your mother-in-law better than I like mine."

"Women will never be equal to men until they can walk down the street with a bald head and a beer gut, and still think they are beautiful."

Underlying such humour is a genuine sense of incomprehension. Both men and women find their opposite gender perplexing, and often the source of chauvinist or feminist ridicule.

It almost goes without saying, that the relationships between men and women have undergone the most remarkable of all the social revolutions in the twentieth century. At the beginning of the last century, role relationships were fairly straightforward. The best education was given to the male in the household. It was he who went out to earn a living. Women stayed at home, kept the house in order and reared the children. Many things have changed. I can think of at least three revolutions:

- The capability of the woman is proven to be equal to the man. Woman have equal choice in education, career and social standing. In the twentieth century we have witnessed the first female Prime Minister, the introduction of female clergy in the Church of England, female high court judges, corporate executives and so on. The maxim 'it's no job for a woman' seemed to be made in order to be broken.
- The advent of safe and reasonably successful contraception has enabled women to make planned choices about when, if and how many children they may be able to have.[1]
- Cultural attitudes have changed. It is no longer assumed that men and women will fulfil stereotypical roles in home and society. For example, it is not uncommon for husbands to stay at home to care for the children while the woman pursues her career (although recent surveys have also revealed that women still do the majority of looking after children and housework, while men do the majority of DIY).

For many people, the evident equality and capability of men and women puts them at odds with the traditional Bible teaching. The logical consequence of these changes, so it is argued, means that Paul's teaching on role-relationships is no longer relevant.

One difficultly with this way of thinking is that Paul does not base his understanding of the role-relationships of men and women on the, admittedly un-emancipated, prevailing *culture* around him, but rather upon the biblical view of *creation*. Paul's argument in Ephesians 5 seems to be that the reason why men and women are placed in such complementary relationships is that behind created differences stands the relationship between God the Father and God the Son. You may like to look at 1 Corinthians 11:3, 8; or 1 Timothy 2:11–15 for examples of this argumentation.

Consequently if you conclude that the Bible no longer speaks to the issue of gender differences today, then please don't do so on the basis of the large cultural and societal changes. This has never been the way in which the Bible has argued. The issue for me becomes whether the Bible is to be trusted on this matter, as with any other matter it speaks about authoritatively.

It is often assumed that the Bible teaches a hierarchical view of the role relationships of men and women. This view assumes that the Bible teaches that men are authoritive over women, implying their superiority, and women are to be subordinate to them and inferior. This seems to me to be alien to the New Testament way of thinking.[2]

Before we begin week 3 of the Diamond Marriage Course I ask the couples to read Ephesians 5:21–33. Many of them have already had a lively discussion about the contents of the passage before we get to our evening meeting! Does it not seem so outdated and, even unchristian, to expect wives to submit to their husbands? Many of the wives hold down responsible jobs in management and leadership. Most of the husbands consider themselves reasonably liberated from chauvinism, and expect to share the roles of childrearing and domestic chores.

So, as we begin the evening, many of them have come spoiling for a fight!

I begin by encouraging them to reaffirm their commitment to sit 'under God's word' not 'over God's word'. I also restate my conviction that God's word is not only true, but good. While our society has been concerned to throw out the mucky bathwater of male chauvinism and female inequality, at some point, it seems to me, the baby (call it male/female complementarity) flew through the air as well.

In an attempt to defuse the atmosphere, we look at what the Bible expects of the husband, first. The husband is encouraged to love his wife as Christ loved the Church and gave himself up for her (see Eph. 5:25). I can't think of a wife who wouldn't be delighted if her husband loved her in that way!

I hope, by this point, the couples are at least prepared to give the Bible a fair hearing, and not to dismiss what it says out of hand. Next, we consider some of the books on male/female relationships which can be bought at any high street bookshop. They are worthy of a brief survey now.

Changes in popular perceptions about male/female marital roles

In the last decade, there have been several popular books published on the apparently startling discovery that men and women are different! It has long been assumed that men and women are equal in value and dignity. But it has only recently been reaffirmed that they are in fact very different.

You may have seen some of these popular titles in airport bookshops. *Men Are from Mars, Women Are from Venus* imagines the inhabitants of Mars meeting up with the residents of Venus for the first time. Men and women are so different in their outlook on life that they may as well come from different planets!

> Men and Women's values are inherently different... Men mistakenly offer solutions and invalidate feelings, while women offer unsolicited advice and direction... Men and women cope with stress in different ways. While Martians tend to pull away and silently think about what's bothering them, Venusians feel an instinctive need to talk about what's bothering them.[3]

This book humorously examines the different ways in which men and women communicate. It shows the different needs which men and women have for intimacy.

In another popular book, *Why Men Don't Listen and Women Can't Read Maps*, the authors joke about this difference. You will never hear a man say, 'Hey, Frank, I'm going to the toilet, you wanna come with me'! Men dominate TV remote controls. They don't ask for directions when lost. Why these differences?, the authors ask:

> The biological evidence now available, however, shows convincingly that it is our hormones and brain wiring that are largely responsible for our attitudes, preferences and behaviour... Difference is not the opposite of equality. Equality means being free to choose to do the things we want to do and difference means that, as men or women, we may not want to do the same things. We usually choose different things off the same list.[4]

The book offers some explanations for common gender differences. They seek to explain:

- Why men really can't do more than one thing at a time
- Why women make such a mess of reverse parallel parking
- Why women talk so much and men so little
- Why men love erotic images and women aren't impressed
- Why men offer solutions but hate advice
- Why women despair about men's silences
- Why men want sex and women need love.[5]

Why Men Don't Iron. The Real Science of Gender Studies also challenges the dominant view in the 1990s that male/female differences are conditioned by societal expectations. The book, and the accompanying British Channel 4 television series, argues that there are genetic differences which determine the differences in approach which men have from women over food, education, sex and society. Despite a radical feminist agenda, science, they argue, has 'upset the egalitarian applecart by conclusively showing that the sexes are distinct in how they act and think'.[6] Moreover, postmodern thinkers have adopted a mindset which believes that the world was first constructed by men, with female roles in subjection; now it is the turn of women to reverse that trend by undermining male identity.[7]

The assumption of this book is not that 'we are all the same', but rather that we are distinctly different. That to be a man is not to be an inferior version of a woman, nor a better version, but to be what nature intended. This is not to say that a man (or woman) cannot change, but it is to claim that there are constant masculine values.[8]

The book spends some time examining the state of the debate over the level of our behaviour which is determined by our genes.[9] Interestingly, this is the subject of another recent book by the popular psychiatrist, Dr Anthony Clare, *On Men: Masculinity in Crisis*. In this book, Clare examines the impact of testosterone on the social expectations of men. One implication is as follows:

> The problem is one for men and particularly for those men – and they have been the majority – who have defined their lives, their identities, the very essence of their masculinity, in terms of professional and occupational achievement and have prided themselves on the work that only they as men could do... on being providers. Today... married women increasingly reap the benefits of education, harness their intelligence and generate their own incomes. Not merely is the role of provider under siege [for men], the role of father is threatened too... If conception, pregnancy, delivery and childrearing can be perfectly well accomplished without the active participation of the male, then why bother with him at all, given the heartache, the trouble, the sheer cussedness of today's man? Once so proud of his penis... contemporary man now finds he is being reduced to the role of support seed carrier, as women occupy center stage not merely in the creation of new life... but in its nurturing.[10]

With a slightly different twist, A. and B. Moir conclude that the 'new man' should take on his fair share of parenting and household chores, and be in touch with his emotions. However, in the end the Moirs' conclusions and that of Clare are not dissimilar in that they do see an age for the new man: not the old sexism of male dominance, nor the new sexism of feminist dominance, but rather, they argue, we have reached an age of the unsexed.

'The New Man is a biological fantasy, a fancy of the New Woman'.[11] But this is not liberating for men or for women:

> A man can move with the times, he will collect the non-chlorine-bleached Pampers from Mothercare in the four-wheel-drive pickup, and he will even do more. He will love his children, play with them, and enjoy their company, but it is useless and

counter-productive to force him into a unisex frame that denies what he is and tries
to make him what he cannot be. Fathers are not mothers. Men don't iron. And he
has no need to be ashamed of that.[12]

Clare goes on to affirm the need for men to be involved in giving positive male role models, and particularly to be involved in the nurture and training of children too. His conclusions are quite telling:

There is no need to create a 'new man' in the image of woman. There is a need
for the 'old man' to re-emerge. Such a man employs his physical, intellectual and
moral strength not to control others but to liberate himself, not to dominate but to
protect, not to worship achievement but to enlist it in the struggle to find meaning
and fulfillment.[13]

These books offer a fascinating insight into the creative differences between men and women which we observed in Genesis 2. Or, it could be argued, these books are merely realizing the dangers which were involved in jettisoning the prevailing and acknowledged social differences between the sexes. Perhaps these differences were denied in the socially liberating times after the second world war. Whatever is actually the case, it seems a shame that several millennia of social revolution have had to pass before we have come to recognize that God has made us differently, made us for each other, and made us to complement each other. But at the same time we can learn from the advances in science which enable us to observe the created differences between the genders.

Why Men Don't Listen and Women Can't Read Maps also acknowledges the biological evidence which gives a clear picture of why men and women think differently.[14] They argue that this picture shows convincingly that our hormones and brain-wiring are largely responsible for our attitudes, preferences and behaviour.[15] Their contention, along with the other authors mentioned above, is that we need to recognize these differences and not despise them. 'Difference is not the opposite of equality. Equality means being free to choose to do things we want to do and difference means that, as men or women, we may not want to do the same things'.[16]

My point here is that what may seem to be very obvious to people steeped in a Judaeo-Christian heritage, comes across as radically countercultural to postmodern ears. Perhaps the pendulum is swinging back.

The Surrendered Wife, looks at the gender revolution from the perspective of the woman, not the man.[17] This book, as the title implies, makes some radical suggestions – at least radical for our postmodern age – on the role of women.

Laura Doyle comments on how her marriage was collapsing until she learned to surrender. 'Today I call myself a surrendered wife because when I stopped trying to control the way John did everything and started trusting him implicitly, I began to have the marriage I've always dreamed of.'[18]

She argues that when she stopped bossing her husband around, giving him advice and criticizing, a new union emerged. 'The man who wooed me was back'.[19] She uses the analogy of ballroom dancing, which requires two equally skilful dancers (of opposite sex) to work together in harmony. However, it is painfully obvious that one must lead and the other must follow.[20]

The positives pointed out by this book resonate well with the wisdom of Ephesians 5. In this passage the wife is told to submit to her husband; the husband is told to love. Each partner is encouraged to look out for the other's rights, and the passage implicitly promises that each partner in turn will find their own needs met. Doyle particularly has in mind encouraging women to treat their husbands with the respect and trust that they expect. To wives reading her book Doyle says:

> I am not saying that *you* are responsible for every problem in your marriage. You are not. Your husband has plenty of areas he could improve too, but that's nothing you can control. You can't make him change – you can only change yourself... Rather than wasting time thinking about what my husband should do, I prefer to keep all my energy for improving *my* happiness.[21]

This book may provide the motivation for change, but again we notice that Ephesians 5 promises the power to do so. When a husband loves as Christ loves the church and a wife submits to her husband as to the Lord, they find that they are not alone in the process, but enabled to live in the way that most glorifies God. Christ models giving and receiving of such love in his relationship with his bride, the church, and following his example does give happiness and joy.

What are we to make of the conclusions of these modern books? Surely, it seems to me, we are to conclude that the creation principles of Genesis 2:24 continue to echo in human hearts down the centuries. The search for intimacy, purpose, procreation, and yes, joy, is best found in the complementary roles of male and female in marriage.

But our interest in this subject also goes beyond a human sociological concern. It is a peculiarly recent phenomenon created by our western culture that has come to view family in the isolation of a closed domestic unit with Mum, Dad and children. My question is not only: Should we view family as more than that? But does the Bible have something to say about the created purpose of male and female in marriage? What makes the Christian marriage *Christian*?

The Dynamics of Biblical Complementarity

In this part of the book we are considering what it means to think of our marriage as a triangle. In other words, we are not just looking at the horizontal relationship between a husband and a wife. Rather, we are thinking about their relationship as a triangle, with God as the central and uniting focus of their marriage. This focus on God comes out in Ephesians 5: 'Wives submit to your husband *as to the Lord*' (v. 22); 'Husbands, love your wives, *just as Christ loved the church*' (v. 25).

Obviously, we have already spoken quite a bit about God's involvement in the couple's relationship. After all it is he who created men and women and has told them how to relate to each other. However, in this section we want to think about what the triangle looks like. In other words, it is my hope that we will be able to move beyond observable differences between men and women, and see how having Christ at the apex of the marriage will help us relate to each other as we ought.

Despite the large number of paperbacks extolling the different and complementary relationship between the sexes, there are few solutions offered by the books I have just reviewed as to *how*, having acknowledged our differences, we may use these differences to enhance our relationship. It seems to me that we will not relate rightly to each other in marriage, until we include Christ as the head of the relationship. Only he gives us the power to change.

This agrees with the central theme of Ephesians. John Stott describes the theme of the book as 'God's new society'. This is not society as we know it. Rather it is a society made up of people who have been saved by grace through faith in the Lord Jesus Christ, made up of Jews and Gentiles (and people of all kinds of backgrounds) who have come to peace with God and thereby peace with one another.It is a society which finds itself located in different cultures in the world, at times at odds with the standards of the world, and waiting for the day when God will take its members to be with the king of this society, Jesus.

From Ephesians 5:22–6:4 Paul gives the 'Household Rules' for the members of God's society. These verses include instructions on how we are to conduct ourselves in marriage, family life and work.

John Stott wisely warns:

> We have to be very careful not to overstate this biblical teaching on authority. It does not mean that the authority of husbands, parents and masters is unlimited, or that wives, children and workers are required to give unconditional obedience. No, the submission required is to God's authority delegated to human beings. If, therefore they misuse their God-given authority (e.g. by commanding what God forbids or forbidding what God commands), then our duty is no longer conscientiously to submit, but conscientiously to refuse to do so. For, to submit in such circumstances would be to disobey God. The principle is clear: we must submit right up to the point where obedience to human authority would involve disobedience to God.[22]

Imagine a familiar scenario. A couple meet, like each other, fall in love, decide to get engaged, prepare to be married, enjoy a wedding day and honeymoon and spend the rest of their life together.

Imagine this less familiar scenario. Paul stretches our minds with lofty themes here. God presides over a long courtship between his Son and his future daughter-in-law, the church! In Ephesians, the human married relationship gives an example of how God is preparing for a great wedding festival at the end of time between his Son (the bridegroom) and the church (his bride).

Think of the preparation that goes into getting ready for a wedding day! There are bookings to be made, invitations to be sent out, a reception to be organized, flowers to be arranged, a honeymoon to be booked, and so the list goes on. In this passage, Paul tells us that God has been preparing for that end-time marriage since before the creation of the world and one day the whole world will witness this wedding! The unity between Christ and the church will bring about a unity between all things in heaven and on earth at the end of time (see Eph. 1:9–10; 3:7–12).

Christian marriage helps prepare the way for that great end-time day when a couple's human marriage will look like the marriage which is to come. How does a Christian couple build their marriage with Christ at the centre? How can their human marriage best image and anticipate the future marriage of Christ and his bride?

The primary principle at work in Ephesians 5:21–33 is that in order to love their spouse properly they each need to love *beyond* their partner. Much of this understanding of Ephesians 5 has come from my reading of Jonathan Edwards (more about him later).

Perhaps I can use a simple illustration. I have been given a helpful piece of advice which has improved my golf putting! A common weakness when on the green is to putt the ball on line with the hole, but to have the ball trickle to a halt before it plops home. It's called 'choking on the ball'. A helpful remedy is to think in terms of hitting about 3–4 inches beyond the hole. This helps sustain the ball to the point where it will drop in the hole.

In a similar way, the only way in which we can reach the target of loving our spouse the way the Bible expects, is to love *beyond* them. If we make Christ the target of our love then we will love them as he expects too! If we fail to do that our love will regularly stop short of the biblical ideal, and will grind to a halt before it reaches its intended target. Hopefully it will never end in choking the spouse!

Voluntary Deference

'Wives, submit to your husbands as to the Lord' (v. 22)

There are two things which need to be noticed in this verse. First, the submission required of the wife is voluntary. This is not a verse to be used by husbands to berate their wife. She has to look after her responsibilities and he has to look after his (ironically, of course, as we shall see, when both of them do this, they find their own needs met too). The passage does not say, 'husbands make your wife submit to you'; nor, 'wives make your husband love you'.

Second, Paul does not tell the wife to *obey* her husband. The word used here (*hupotassō*, meaning to be subject or subordinate, in the sense of a voluntary yielding) is different to the word used in Ephesians 6:1 (here the word comes from *hypakouō* meaning to obey, as a slave would obey a master). Children are to obey their parents. The wife, however, is not called to a blind obedience of her husband. Remember, the husband is encouraged to 'love, cherish and worship'. The wife is encouraged to 'love, cherish and obey'.[23]

The context of this verse is the mutual submission expected of every Christian (5:21). The fivefold evidence of being filled with the Holy Spirit includes submitting to each other ('speak to one another in psalms, hymns and spiritual songs. Sing and make music in your heart to the Lord, always giving thanks to God the Father for everything, in the name of our Lord Jesus Christ. Submit to one another out of reverence for Christ' vv. 19–21). The wife does this by submitting. The husband does this by loving.

It is popular to say that Paul insists that both husband and wife submit to each other. At one level, of course, they are required to do that, as verse 21 indicates. But it seems, from the flow of the passage, that the way in which each submits to the other is outlined in the paragraphs that follow verse 21.

We noted above that both partners are called upon to look out for *each other's* rights. However, it is important to notice that the kind of self-sacrificial love, to which each is called, is expressed differently. It would be inappropriate to reverse the wording of this text to read: 'The husband is to submit to the wife in all things… The wife is to love as Christ loved the church'. If we are in any doubt, substituting Christ and the church would obviously be inappropriate: 'Wives love your husbands as the church loved Christ and gave herself up for him…' Such a reversal of verse 25 would be blasphemy. Clearly Paul is not speaking about an identical submission between husband and wife. There is some distinction in roles between the two of them.

You will remember that we have already seen in Genesis 2 that men and women are made equal but are in a relationship of headship and submission. No suitable helper was found for Adam in the animal kingdom, and God made Eve especially for that role. When Eve was presented to Adam, he made a joyful response which we paraphrased as: 'Out of my rib – at last - bone of my bones and flesh of my flesh!' We also noticed that Adam names her, as he had the animals. This would seem to suggest some leading or authoritive role over her.

I mention this because, the reason why men and women struggle so much with the teaching in Ephesians 5 is not because headship and submission have been introduced as a result of the fall. Rather, the fall resulted in the perversion of a healthy complementarity (headship became rule, and submission became frustration, see Genesis 3).

Moreover, neither the husband nor the wife will be able to 'love and submit' in this way if they don't see the perfect Lord behind their imperfect partner (v. 22, v. 25). This is where the triangular structure of marriage becomes so important.

The popular books on marriage I mentioned earlier are perceptive in their observations of the differences between men and women. However, I do not believe that they help us to work well with our differences to complement and build each other up. Ephesians does! What these books do reveal to me is that our society is despairing of a radical feminism which has said that equal worth means equal role. We are also despairing of a male chauvinism which fails to value and affirm women in their complementary roles.

In order for a wife to look to her husband to lead the relationship, she needs first to look *beyond* her husband to her Lord. Wives, love Jesus most, and you will also love your husband best. Having the husband lead and love her this way does not mean that he should not fully involve her in all decisions in the family, nor that he should take the lead in every area of the marriage.

However, in my experience, many wives do look for a godly, proactive lead from their husbands (who often fail to give it). They expect and hope that the husband will be active in all the affairs of the family. But, they can be inclined to do a lot of the 'running' in making big decisions and then expect the husband to own the decisions and carry the responsibility for them. Alternatively, they can be inclined to give over areas of decision-making, but quickly take them back again. Many of these situations arise because the husband is, perhaps, failing to lead, or leading in an unhelpful manner (we shall think more about this in a minute). For now, let us notice what this verse does say: Wives, take up a submissive posture when a clear lead is required.

Car journeys can be very instructive about our gender relationships. I am not *just* talking about the husband's reluctance to ask for directions! Wives, what are you like as a passenger in the car? Are your finger nails embedded in the dash board when you husband is driving? Do you depress your foot on an imaginary brake every time you come to a junction? Back-seat driving can be a real problem in the marriage relationship too. Wives need to resist the temptation to 'grab the wheel' in the relationship, or to manipulate the direction of big decisions from behind the scenes.

Lest this teaching seems too demanding or unfair, we need to look at the expectations the Bible has for the husband's love of his wife. On three occasions husbands are told to love their wives (Eph. 5:25, 28, 33). It would have been quite a shock for the original readers of Paul's letter to hear that the husband is not told to lord or subjugate his wife, which would have been the expectation of a hierarchical society.

Sacrificial Giving

'Husbands, love your wives, just as Christ loved the church' (v. 25).

How exactly did Christ show his love for the church? We know that he didn't buy her flowers, take her on a date, or do the laundry for a change! The love that is being extolled here is not primarily to do with small self-denials, nor even, primarily 'feeling' love (although strong feelings are expected to go with it). Rather, this love has to do with total self-sacrifice.

And, lest this language be misunderstood, it also involves finding one's own needs met, in the context of a sincere desire to see his wife flourish and bloom. The husband's love is described as being sacrificial (v. 25), sanctifying (vv. 26–27), and even includes 'self-love' (vv. 28–30).

Actually, the way in which husbands love their wives is analogous to the expectations of Christian discipleship. Love is not inconsistent with radical self-sacrifice. D. Bonhoeffer famously wrote: 'When Christ calls a man, he bids him come and die'.[24]

My point here is that the husband also needs to look *beyond* his wife to Christ if he is going to fulfil his obligations. He too will 'choke the ball' if he doesn't aim beyond the target! In order to love this way, he must look to Christ's headship over the church. Headship is not at odds with love. Indeed, Christ loved the Church and liberated her, by exercising his servant-headship over her (see Eph. 4:15ff., for example).

A husband should love his wife by the kind of self-sacrifice which liberates her to be the person she should be. He will only be able to do this if he keeps Christ in view as his model lover. This is the standard. Martin Lloyd Jones comments:

> How many of us have realised that we are always to think of the married state in terms of the doctrine of the atonement? Is that our customary way of thinking of marriage? Where do we find what the books have to say about marriage? Under which section? Under ethics. But it does not belong there. We must consider marriage in terms of the doctrine of the atonement.[25]

The allusion in Ephesians 5:25–27 is to the bridal bath which the beloved had before her wedding ceremony, and the splendid dress she wore on the day. The inference of these verses is that the husband's job is to 'make her day' – not just her wedding day, but every day.

If the wife is called to give up everything by submitting to her husband, the husband is called to an equally high self-sacrifice. Both parties are to look, not to their own rights, but to the interests of their spouse. The wife wants nothing more than to be loved sacrificially by her husband, but because of the fall the husband will be inclined to domineer (Gen. 3:16b). On the other hand the husband, rather than actively and sacrificially loving his wife, will be inclined to abdicate his responsibility in the same way Adam was silent in the garden and refused to take the blame for their sin (Gen. 3:1–6, 12). Larry Crabb perceptively comments on this verse:

> The silence of Adam is the beginning of every man's failure, from the rebellion of Cain to the impatience of Moses, from the weakness of Peter down to my failure yesterday to love my wife well.... Since Adam every man has had a natural inclination to remain silent when he should speak.[26]

If the wife's temptation is to 'grab the wheel' or manipulate from behind, the husband's temptation is to abdicate his responsibility. Husbands, don't grunt from behind the newspaper, but lead. Don't be a silent, Adam, speak up and show the love which is extolled here.

The husband is called to give to his wife. This is not primarily about *things*, such as a home or income, but to give of *himself*. He is to resist the temptation to hold back, either by abdicating his role, or by tyrannizing his wife (more on these issues in the next chapter).

Intimate Caring

'Husbands love your wives as you love your own body' (vv. 28-29)

The implication of these verses is that couple are no longer two distinct people, but one. Paul pushes the 'one flesh' analogy to make his point. He states, 'No one ever hates his body' (v. 29). Christ loved his body, the church, by sacrificing and caring for it. So too husbands should love their 'one flesh' partner as their own body. Now, I realize that you probably object to this statement: 'I hate my body', you may say. Maybe you look in the mirror and say 'Yuck!'

It is worth pointing out, though, that it is men Paul is addressing here. We men are far more likely to look in the mirror, flex our biceps, push out our chest and turn to the side nodding our head in silent approval of the toning effect of a few extra sessions in the gym.

Paul's point is: we love ourselves naturally. When our body needs washing, we wash it. When our body needs feeding, we feed it. When our body needs caring for, we care for it. We do all we can to avoid pain and we do everything we can to love, pamper, groom, cherish and comfort our bodies. And if our bodies could speak in our defense, they would say, 'I want for nothing!' There is an instinctive care which we already show for ourselves which should now become part of the care the husband shows to his wife. Husband and wife are one flesh and everything the husband instinctively does for his body, he should now do for his beloved.

Joyful Anticipation

'Husbands and wives, anticipate the joyful completion of Christ's work in your marriage' (v. 32).

Agatha Christie once said, 'The best husband a woman could ask for is an archeologist, because the older she gets the more interested he gets in her!' Actually, our increasing interest in our wife is not just because she is 'maturing', but rather because Christ's work in her will be subsumed in a greater purpose for the whole of the church. The moment of completion of Christ's work will be the final presentation of his bride, the church, to the Lord. This will, in fact, be our theme in Chapter 5. But, a sense of joyful anticipation should shape and mould the outlook of the marriage now.

God is making a church which will be pure and without spot or blemish (Rev. 19:7–9). To this extent marriage is transitory. For, at the resurrection there will be no more marrying or giving in marriage. There is an aspect of marriage which is passing and will be caught up in the final consummation of all things (Mark 12:25).

We have already noted that the 'mystery' Paul speaks of is not primarily the marriage relationship, neither is the mystery just the allegorical picture of the church's marriage to Christ. Rather, the mystery is that God should create marriage in order to give the world a living, breathing illustration of his cosmic purposes! Godly marriages serve Gospel purposes! For husbands to love like Christ, they too need to look beyond their wife, to Christ, who will soon complete his work in both his wife and the church. God will finish this work when he has brought all things together under the unity of Christ the head (Eph. 1:10).

Summary and Implications

Earlier we asked how joy could be revived in dutiful, but loveless marriages. Here in Ephesians 5 we have begun to see some answers in considering the triangle part of the Diamond Marriage.

We have spent some time looking at how God expects the husband and wife to relate to each other:

- Wives, we are told, can learn how to love their husbands by looking at the kind of love which the church shows to Christ (responding love).
- Husbands can learn to love their wives by looking at the kind of love which Christ showed to the church (initiating, self-sacrificial love).

The wife may learn to love when she looks at the church's relationship with Christ, the head. The husband may learn to love when he looks at Christ's relationship with the church.

The effect of sin needs to be taken seriously, and can be summarized as follows:

> In the home, the husband's loving humble headship tends to be replaced by domination or passivity; the wife's intelligent, willing submission, tends to be replaced by usurpation or servility.[27]

But when sin is recognized and renounced, joy follows!

Joy will be revived in marriage when:

- Both partners seek the joy of their beloved by responding to each other as Ephesians suggests.
- Both partners enjoy the dynamics of the complementary relationship which God has made.
- Both partners love beyond their partner, and see God as the source and goal of all true love.

Don't 'choke' your marriage, focus beyond your partner and on Christ!

In the next chapter we shall spend some time considering how we can work out these principles in the practicalities of domestic life, communication and sex.

---

[1] It is interesting to notice the changes made to the Marriage Service in recent years. There appears to be a development in the Anglican theology of marriage from the 1662 Book of Common Prayer service (where

procreation is put first) through the Alternative Services Book (1980) service to Common Worship (2000). The preface to these latter services emphasizes companionship. The modern protestant church has freely accepted the idea that sex is a 'good' in itself, even when procreation cannot happen.

[2] This view also necessitates assuming that Christ is an inferior relationship to God the Father. In fact, with 1 Corinthians 11:1–3 in mind, we have the clearest suggestion that it is possible to hold a submissive role with no assumption of inferiority, for that is precisely what the Son demonstrates in his relationship with his Father.

[3] J. Gray, *Men are From Mars, Women are From Venus*, London: Harper Collins, p. 11.

[4] A. and B. Pease, *Why Men Don't Listen and Women Can't Read Maps*, London: Orien Books, 2001, pp. 7–9.

[5] They have subsequently published another book on the subject entitled, *Why Men Lie and Women Cry*, London: Orien, 2002.

[6] A. and B. Moir, *Why Men Don't Iron: The Real Science of Gender Studies*, London: Harper Collins, 1998, p. 13.

[7] Moir, *Why Men Don't Iron*, p.18.

[8] Moir, *Why Men Don't Iron*, p. 21.

[9] Moir, *Why Men Don't Iron*, pp. 41–51.

[10] A. Clare, *On Men: Masculinity in Crisis*, London: Arrow Books, 2001, pp. 7-8.

[11] Moir, *Why Men Don't Iron*, p.275.

[12] Moir, *Why Men Don't Iron*, p. 274.

[13] Moir, *Why Men Don't Iron*, p. 221.

[14] Pease, *Why Men Don't Listen and Women Can't Read Maps*.

[15] Pease, *Why Men Don't Listen and Women Can't Read Maps*, p. 6.

[16] Pease, *Why Men Don't Listen and Women Can't Read Maps*, p. 9.

[17] 45 L. Doyle, *The Surrendered Wife*, London: Simon and Schuster, 2001.

[18] Doyle, *The Surrendered Wife*, p. 14.

[19] Doyle, *The Surrendered Wife*, p. 18.

[20] Doyle, *The Surrendered Wife*, p. 20.

[21] Doyle, *The Surrendered Wife*, p. 25.

[22] J. Stott, *God's New Society*, Leicester: IVP, 1979, pp. 218f.

[23] Presumably the reason why the word 'obey' is used in the marriage service is because some translations render 1 Peter 3:1 as 'wives obey your husbands'. But even here, notice that the motivation behind the call for wives to 'be subject' to their husbands (3:1) is in order that the non-believing husband may be won over by her godly behaviour, not in order that he may treat her as inferior.

[24] D. Bonhoeffer, *The Cost of Discipleship*, London: SCM Press, p. 79.

[25] M. Lloyd Jones, *Ephesians: Life in the Spirit*, Banner of Truth, 1974, p. 148.

[26] L. Crabb, *The Silence of Adam*, Grand Rapids: Zondervan Publishing House, 1995, p. 12.

[27] *The Danvers Statement*, Affirmation 4, published by the Council on Biblical Manhood and Womanhood, 2825 Lexington Road, Box 926, Louisville, KY 40280, USA.

4

WORKING THE ANGLES

In the previous chapter we likened Christian marriage to a triangle involving husband, wife and the Lord. In order for the horizontal relationship between husband and wife to be healthy and joyful, the Lord needs to be unseen partner in every relationship.

We also noticed, in Ephesians 5, that the motivation behind the wife's submission towards her husband is christological (v. 22, as to the Lord), and it is ecclesiological (v. 24, as the church submits to Christ so the wife should submit to the husband). The motivation behind the husband's love for his wife is ecclesiological (v. 25, he is to love her as Christ loved the church); it is redemptive (v. 26, through 'the washing of the word' – more on this in a moment); and, it includes healthy self-interest (v. 28, he loves her as he loves his own body).

A good example of the latter point may be seen in the film *As Good as it Gets* (1997). Melvin Udall (played by Jack Nicholson) is an egocentric writer with an obsessive-compulsive disorder. His neighbour asks him to look after his dog while he goes into hospital. Combine this with the frustration of having the only waitress who can cope with fulfilling his outrageous breakfast requirements, Carol (played by Helen Hunt), having to leave work to look after her son, and Melvin is in torment!

There is a little reminiscence of Charles Dickens' *Christmas Carol* here, the scrooge-like Melvin's life is turned around, not by four ghosts, but by Carol and a dog. The film poses the apparent egocentricity, even of true love. When Melvin begins to fall in love with Carol, they are both worried that the best compliment which he can pay her is how *he* feels when he is around her. Gradually, as the film unfolds, Carol manages to move from tolerating this eccentric, to loving him, despite all his quirks. Melvin moves beyond a selfish self-absorption to actually loving her. However, they both gradually come to realize that to compliment someone for how you feel when you are with them is actually a *great* compliment. For self-interest, it seems, is not entirely absent from true love.

It is sometimes said, 'opposites attract'. This may be true, and many people actively look for a complementary counterpart in their marriage partner. We have also already observed that there is some truth in the truism, 'like attracts like'. One implication of the these statements is that I am very aware that no two marriages look the same. I do not want to be prescriptive in this chapter. I have encountered many different couples who put these verses into practice, each of whom is as different as the uniqueness of every human being. This is also a private issue to be worked out in every Christian home. However, it does seem to me that the Bible is clear in assuming that God has designed marriage to work in a certain way. In both Ephesians 5 and Genesis 1–2 we have noticed that God wants the husband to play a more initiating role in the relationship. He wants the wife to play a more responding role. Unfortunately, since each of us is tainted by sin, God's good design is corrupted. But Christian marriages do well to find ways to work out God-given role relationships with Christ as the head of the home. In practice, I have come across many joyless marriages caused by passive husbands and overbearing, pushy wives. And I have come across an equal number of joyless marriages caused by chauvinistic and aggressive husbands, with compliant and weak wives.

John Piper summarizes the interplay between 'headship' and 'submission' in Christian marriage:

> At the heart of mature masculinity is a sense of benevolent responsibility to lead, provide for and protect women in ways appropriate to a man's differing relationships.
>
> At the heart of mature femininity is a freeing disposition to affirm, receive and nurture strength and leadership from worthy men in ways appropriate to a woman's differing relationships.[1]

Working out some of the practicalities which flow from the last chapter clearly involves working on the three dimensions of the triangle of which Ephesians 5:21ff. speaks.

Francis Schaeffer is surely right when he says, 'True Spirituality covers all of reality... In this sense there is nothing concerning reality that is not spiritual.'[2] Consequently, problems of communication, sexual fulfilment, love, sacrifice and spiritual compatibility are all spiritual problems. The early church rejected the Gnostic separation of body and soul, but all-to-often the modern church has assumed that matters to do with the body are less spiritual than matters of the soul.

The Bible does have some very practical advice to offer in each of these areas. However it is not a spiritual equivalent to *Men Are from Mars, Women Are from Venus*, or a relationship manual. Rather, the Bible gives a pattern (of initiating and responding) which is manifested in the husband–wife relationship, and shown more fully in Christ's relationship with his church.

Preparation Questions

The Husband's Initiating Love

The husband needs to evaluate his love in the light of Christ's love for the church as outlined in the three main ways listed in the previous chapter:[3]

- First, the husband needs to do self-sacrificial things for the sake of his wife. This may mean giving up some hobby or activity if it takes away from the intimacy of the marriage or, more positively, being the servant-leader in the household. Is your life self-sacrificial towards your wife?

- Second, the husband needs to be aware of the danger of thinking of love purely in terms of action, and not in terms of affection (see reading project below). Do you consider that your feelings towards your wife matter?

- Third, do you see yourself as a redeemer to your wife? I don't mean this in terms of being her saviour, only Christ can do that. Rather, do you consider the ways in which you can free her to be the person God wants her to be, to so love her as to liberate her?

- Fourth, do you seek your joy in your spouse? Have you appreciated that duty is not enough? God wants you to find joy in your wife. How do you seek to 'please your wife'? (see 1 Cor. 7:33–34)

The Wife's Responsive Submission

The wife needs to evaluate her love in view of the way in which the church submits to Christ:

- First, what are some of the common perceptions of submission which make this teaching difficult in contemporary culture? How do you work out the initiating/responding relationship in your marriage?
- Second, study Proverbs 31:10–31 together. Does this 'excellent wife' surprise you? How do the principles of submission work out in this marriage?
- Third, in what ways do you feel that you and your spouse relate complementarily? Are there areas where you are too similar or have clashes of authority/responsibility? In the light of the previous chapter on Ephesians 5, how are you going to resolve these issues?
- Fourth, it is sometimes observed that husbands are too passive in decision-making in the home; wives are too active in decision-making. Is this the case in your relationship?

Husband and Wife Together

- Try to evaluate your time, together and apart, before the Lord. Are there parts of your marriage where the lordship of Jesus is not being worked out in any of these areas?
  - o Time commitments?
  - o Prayer over big or little issues?
  - o Church involvement?
  - o Discipline and nurture of the children?
  - o Corporate and individual Bible reading?
- How is it evident in your household that Christ is the head of the family?

Practical implications

Sex – Initiating and Responding

'For this reason a man will leave his father and mother and be united to his wife, and the two will become one flesh.' However, each one of you also must love his wife as he loves himself, and the wife must respect her husband (Eph. 5:31 and 33).

For the husband and wife to be *one flesh* involves more than just their sexual relationship, but it is certainly not less than that. It must include the sensual and sexual part of the relationship. In sex, men and women are reconnected as *one flesh* again, in complementary union. This is more than the physical act, it is the union and intermeshing of two lives – so that we hardly know where one person ends and the other begins. They have become 'one'. Love-making and procreation, like all of God's created gifts, 'is good' (cf. 1 Tim. 4:4–5).

Physical and Emotional

Physically, the husband and wife 'fit' together naturally. The man's sexual organ is intended for the female sexual organ.

Satisfying sexual experiences occur in the context in which God intended. In the first instance this assumes a lifelong, monogamous marriage. This is so clear in the Bible, but so counter-cultural today! The entertainment media asserts again and again that fulfilling sex is to be found in physical arousal unfettered by long-term commitment to a relationship. The Bible's testimony that physical pleasure is found in a committed relationship is, actually, the experience of happily married couples. It is no mistake that the word 'know' in the Bible is a shorthand for sexual relationships. We need this knowledge in order to enjoy God's good gift. We need the exclusive intimacy which only lifelong marriage can offer.[4]

In the physical act of love-making, the husband is usually the initiator. He woos and entices his wife. He comes inside of her and she envelopes him. It is more often than not the case, that the husband will need to be proactive in enticing his wife, and, she is more likely to respond when his advances begin long before bedtime! Through thoughtful words and actions, through non-sexual physical touch, the pathway to sexual relationship is opened up.

I am not an expert in knowing how to solve physical sexual problems. It may be that a discussion with a doctor or counsellor will give help when certain sexual problems exist.[5] What I do know, though, is that many issues of sexual frustration are not physical, but emotional and spiritual. When love-making happens in the context of acceptance, trust and free self-giving, issues of orgasm, arousal and impotence are often dealt with.

For both couples, the principle of initiating and responding applies in the bedroom, as well as in other areas of marriage. Joy, satisfaction and real intimacy are found when each couple concentrates on bringing joy and fulfilment first to their partner and, when they aim to do that they will find satisfaction for themselves as well. Indeed, he who loves his wife, loves himself.

Consider the three main areas of love-making.

Arousal

Clearly, men and women are aroused very differently. For the man, sight plays a big part of it. So, for his eyes only, a wife will excite and arouse her husband through what she wears, and how she regards her physical appearance. She will need to hear encouragement from her husband that he finds her physically attractive, especially when surrounded by the absolutely unrealistic portrayal of women in the modern media.

Arousal happens very quickly for most men and, in order to provide satisfaction for his wife, the young husband will need to control himself if he is going to prolong love-making to the point where his wife reaches climax.

Most women require a longer period of anticipation before intercourse, this may involve gentle touching, tender words and her husband's attentiveness. Now, my wife was not particularly impressed when I told her that her teeth were like a flock of shorn sheep. But, the Beloved in Solomon's Song of Songs was impressed. Notice the attentive detail which is paid to her physical body. Your wife need not be impressed by your poetry, but your interest in her will arouse her.

Intercourse

The sheer joy of the act of love-making is a consummation of the one flesh union. Again, one wonders at the marvel of the way in which God has created the sexual act – necessary for the propagation of the species – to be the most pleasurable human experience, in a dynamic of giving and receiving love. He woos and enters her; she responds and receives him.

Orgasm

I have read books by Christians which would be ashamed of the – relatively tame – details I am going into here. However, God has not made us like the other animals. The human female does not 'come into heat' where, when penetrated by the male, she will become pregnant. God assumes that the sexual act will be a normal and healthy part of the marriage relationship. Indeed, Paul cautioned that self-denial in this area – something healthy and necessary – should only be for the purpose of spiritual discipline, and by mutual consent (1 Cor. 7:3–5).

Ongoing communication and appropriate experimentation are essential to maintain interest and enjoyment in sex. While orgasm is an essential part for the man, for many women, it is something which needs special attentiveness by her partner. Orgasm is far more than a physical release for the woman. It has to be matched by the feeling of 'being loved', and the woman is generally far from unsatisfied if the latter has happened and the former hasn't. But we note, as many sexual therapists have commented, that the female clitoris seems to perform no other function other than to bring sexual pleasure and, remember Adam's exclamation of joy in Genesis 2:23 and its sexual overtones. A similar excitement is anticipated in Proverbs 5:18ff: 'May your fountain be blessed, and may you rejoice in the wife of your youth. A loving doe, a graceful deer – may her breasts satisfy you always, may you ever be captivated by her love.'

One's religious upbringing can play an enormous part here. If sex has been thought to be 'dirty', or if the woman has felt that it is not appropriate to either initiate or expect personal satisfaction in sex, then there are principles of their complementarity which need to be taught or relearned. This is exacerbated if one or the other partner was not a virgin when they were married. Previous sexual encounters need to be discussed and forgiveness sought, because guilt can play a major part in hindering an open and free relationship.

Communication – Initiating and Responding

There are many different kinds of communication problems which may occur within a marriage. Perhaps the most common refrain I hear is, 'We don't talk any more'. The book *Men Are from Mars, Women Are from Venus* rightly points out that, typically, Martians retreat into their caves, or grunt, when Venusians would rather communicate.

This is exacerbated by the feeling among many men that they come home from work in order to put a distance between themselves and their place of work. Home is their place of retreat, and their family often gets the 'stale leftovers' of their time. However, they can come alive and animated when a phone call for them enquires about football scores or engages them in their favourite pastime topic.

In such instances, remember the dynamic of initiating and responding. Both the husband and wife need to prepare for times when they can talk, without the television on, maybe after children have gone to bed. Perhaps the husband may be better walking around the block once, rather than hurrying home, in order that he is better able to converse when he walks through the door. Similarly, the wife may need to be sensitive to the best times for communicating, and choose those moments well.

Both husbands and wives do well to remember what it was like when first they were dating. Then, they wanted to talk about everything and know every intimate detail. Can you not remember the complaints your parents made over your ability to talk for hours on the phone despite the fact that your boy/girlfriend only left the house minutes earlier? Do you not want to revive that first love?

Husbands and wives also should have individual time pursuing friendships and hobbies. But they should be attentive to their relationship and to allow uncluttered time for communication – probably writing it in the diary in advance!

There is a great danger of stereotyping here, but here are some practical communicationtips:

- Don't talk around things. Do talk through things.
- Find something you enjoy doing together, even if it just going out for coffee or a stroll in the park. But do make a date to do it regularly!
- Be aware of each other's different needs in communication. Often, the woman needs to hear loving words and actions in order to feel loved. The man *does* have emotional needs, but they are, for the most part, different from the woman's.
- A man will often make decisions based on emotional impulse more than the woman will, culturally, however, there is a lot of expectation that men will be emotionally independent.
- The perception of the husband's importance and his success in his career as well as his perceived status among his peers, appear to matter more to men. Whereas, for the wife, relationships among family and friends feature more highly.
- Find some time to talk through these issues.

Busyness, Boredom and Exhaustion – Initiating and Responding

I want to flag up a couple of recurring areas of difficulty in many marriages. I don't have the time to deal with all the issues under each topic, but wish to highlight the ways in which the husband's initiative and the wife's responding helps to address each of them.

Busyness and Exhaustion

In my experience this is a problem for both husband and wife. Our lives seem to be unnecessarily frenetic, and one of the things which gets squeezed out is uncluttered time together. And, even when both of the couple are inhabiting the same physical space and time, they can be so tired or distracted that little genuine communication happens.

The husband should take the initiative in helping bring some order into the domestic diary. This may well mean buying a communal calendar or writing 'dates' in the diary. When the family is young and demands a lot of both parents' time, it is easy to forget that the primary relationship in the household is the husband–wife relationship. If this is given time and space, then the other relationships will have time to flourish too. In my experience, by the time the husband wises up to the pressure which the problems of busyness and exhaustion place upon the marriage, the wife has often given up expecting his initiative in these areas. She will do well to be patient and responsive to any renewed commitment to control the diary.

Boredom

There is some truth in the old adage 'familiarity breeds contempt'. But married couples do well if they celebrate their familiarity, and continue to uncover new interests together. Again, the husband may well be the one to take initiative here, but this should also always be done in consultation, rather than John Wayne-like, expecting a dutiful family to trot on behind!

The greatest relief I felt in watching the film *Lost in Translation* (2004) was that adultery – against all expectations – didn't happen in the end! Fuelled by boredom, sleep deprivation and chance encounter, Bob (played by Bill Murray) and Charlotte (Scarlett Johansson) bump into each other at unsociable hours of the night in the hotel bar. Charlotte's husband is a young, up and coming photographer who has taken his wife to Tokyo while he is photographing a pop band. Bill Murray is there to shoot a single take for a television commercial. For very different reasons they both find themselves abandoned by their other halves and bored. They meet up, flirt and the audience finds itself almost willing them to consummate their relationship! Mercifully, the movie director pulls us up before they do. In fact, he doesn't need to take the relationship 'all the way' because their relationship has transgressed healthy encounter long before the physical side is entertained.

This is a clever film which speaks about the pathway to infidelity. It is a pathway which is fuelled by busyness, opportunity and boredom. Many men I have spoken to about their adultery, have revealed that the separation from their partner, at least initially, had very little to do with sex. Often they were first flattered by the attention of another woman, maybe the excitement of an illicit encounter, and particularly many were glad to have empathetic conversations with someone of the opposite sex.

Couples need to be aware of how subtly affection from a person of the opposite sex can entice away even the apparently most 'safe' marriage partners. Away from home, in the anonymous environment of an after-work pub drink, or a hotel foyer, bored couples may find exciting conversation and genuine attentiveness all-too enticing.

Jonathan and Sarah Edwards

Much of what I have had to say in this book has been influenced by John Piper and, behind him, Jonathan Edwards. Jonathan Edwards has often been dubbed, 'the theologian of joy'. Three hundred years after his death, this New England pastor, and his wife, Sarah, still provide us with a model of joy-filled love which is instructive.

We would do well to look at the way in which Jonathan Edwards interwove the relationship between Love to God, Love to Others and Love to Self. This was evident both in his prolific writings and his loving relationship with his wife, Sarah.

During my reading of Jonathan Edwards, over the last few years, I have been increasingly convinced that his view of biblical love coloured the key relationships of his life. Let me illustrate this briefly in the following two areas which are relevant to our study.

A Marriage of Self-Giving Love
Jonathan and his Wife Sarah

On his deathbed, America's finest theologian saved his dying words for his beloved wife: 'Give my kindest love to my dear wife, and tell her that the uncommon union which has so long subsisted between us has been of such a nature as I trust is spiritual and therefore will continue forever'.[6]

The main study of the Edwards' marriage was made by Elizabeth Dodds.[7] Her work is self-confessedly selective and interested primarily in the human biography of Jonathan and Sarah. Nevertheless, an insight into the Edwards' relationship enables us to appreciate the kind of love in action of which Edwards wrote about extensively.

Jonathan and Sarah Edwards were married on 28 July 1727 at New Haven. They had eleven children. By modern standards, their relationship would have been considerably strained since Edwards would commonly work thirteen hours a day.

> [Sarah Edwards] uniformly paid a becoming deference to her husband and treated him with entire respect, she spared no pains in conforming to his inclinations, and rendering everything in the family agreeable and pleasant: counting it her greatest glory, and that wherein she could best serve God and her generation, to be the means, in this way, of promoting his usefulness and happiness.[8]

Sarah, like many clergy wives, felt keenly the criticism which her husband received. This was especially acute when it came from family sources, such as Chester Williams, an Arminian minister who would turn his head away as he rode past the Edwards' house.[9]

During this period, Sarah Edwards went through a period of depression. She had given birth to their sixth child, their only son, Timothy. Sensing his wife's fatigue, in 1740 Edwards took her on a trip to Boston, without children. The purpose was to have their portraits painted, but with the added benefit of a much needed break from duties.

George Whitefield commented on Jonathan and Sarah Edwards' relationship following his visit to Northampton in 1740:

> A sweeter Couple I have not yet seen... She... talked feelingly and solidly of the Things of God, and seemed to be such a Help meet for her Husband that she caused me to... [pray] God, that he would be pleased to send me a Daughter of Abraham to be my wife.[10]

Jonathan once gave Sarah a gold locket costing £11, an extravagant gift by contemporary standards. He was known to delight in his wife, and while some men went off to ordinations or barn-raisings, Edwards would rather be at home with her whenever he could.

Sarah's way with the children did more for Edwards than shield him from hullabaloo while he studied. The family gave him an incarnate foundation for his ethic. As George Gordon has put it, Edwards' life at home opened up 'the world in which love lifts the whole animal endowment to an ethical level'. In 1738, Edwards poured out his feelings about this in sermons which eventually appeared as a book, *Christian Love as Manifested in the Heart and Life*. He summarized the conviction his family had planted in him that 'the whole world of mankind are chiefly kept in action from day to day... by love'.[11]

Jonathan and his church – sacrificing and serving love

The interrelationship between the analogy of Christ (as bridegroom) and the church (as bride) is carefully woven through Edwards' writing. This joy in marriage is reciprocal: as Christ rejoices in his bride, the bride rejoices in her husband.

In his sermon, 'The church's marriage to her sons, and to her God' Edwards gives clear examples of how this intimate relationship should be worked out:

> The mutual joy of Christ and his church is like that of bridegroom and bride, in that they rejoice in each other as those whom they have chosen above others, for their nearest, most intimate, and everlasting friends and companions...
>
> Christ and his church, like the bridegroom and the bride, rejoice in each other, as those that are the objects of each other's most tender and ardent love. The love of Christ to his church is altogether unparalleled: the height and depth and length and breadth of it pass knowledge: for he loved the church and gave himself for it; and his love to her proved stronger than death. And on the other hand, she loves him with all her heart. Her whole soul is offered up to him in the flame of love.[12]

This picture of Christ and the Church points forward to a day when God will complete his work of bringing his people to glorious perfection. On that day Christ's bride, filled with joy, will be united to her groom.

> And they both in that relation and union, together receive the Father's blessing; and shall thenceforward rejoice together, in consummate, uninterrupted, immutable, and everlasting glory, in the love and embraces of each other and joint enjoyment of the love of the Father.[13]

Edwards goes on to apply this analogy to the role of the pastor as being like a husband, sacrificing and serving the congregation, giving himself to provide the church comfort and welfare. Accordingly, the church is to submit to the pastor as unto Christ. The results of a faithful union between pastor and church is joy, helpfulness and a working together for the good of each other.

Much of Jonathan Edwards' writing is quite difficult to read and understand. In the section of his Works on *True Virtue* he ponders, 'How broad can self-love be before it ceases to be selfish?' To which he answers, love cannot be said to be complete unless it extends upwards towards God as the ground of love and outwards towards human beings as the goal of love.

Such discussion takes us beyond our focus on Ephesians 5. However, it is significant to observe that Paul assumes that loving our wife selflessly is actually loving ourselves (v. 28). At one level this is because of the dynamics of the 'one flesh' relationship we have been considering. At another level this self-interest in marriage is appropriate and fulfilling when the husband and wife have God as the *ground* of true love, that is, their love is enabled by and empowered by God. Also, God is to be the *goal* of true love – so that the husband sees beyond his wife to Christ, the head of the marriage.

It seems to me that Jonathan and Sarah Edwards provide us with a living illustration of how such true love is to be manifested.[14]

Summary and Conclusion

This chapter is not intended to deal exhaustively with marital problems. There are plenty of helpful books cited in the footnotes which will assist if required.

What we have tried to do is to provide a model of 'initiating and responding' (in line with our understanding of Ephesians 5:22–33) in which the husband and wife take their respective roles seriously. This recognizes that they are not in competition with each other; neither are they clones of each other. Rather, they are creative counterparts to each other and they will be much stronger if they recognize that! When we are liberated from the social stereotypes imposed by our culture we shall be free to be who we are, gloriously made in the image of God, and redeemed by the saving work of Christ!

---

[1] J. Piper, *What's the Difference? Manhood and Womanhood Defined According to the Bible*, Westchester: Crossway, 1990, p. 18.

[2] F. Schaeffer, *A Christian Manifesto*, Westchester: Crossway, 1984.

[3] Sacrificial giving (Ephesians 5:25), intimate caring (vv.28-29), joyful anticipation (v.22).

[4] A very helpful and practical book on this subject is LaHaye, *The Act of Marriage*. Chapter 13 includes an extensive survey of 2,300 Christian married couples, concluding among other things (and contrary to common perceptions), that Christian couples comment on far higher sexual satisfaction than their non-Christian counterparts.

[5] See also, LaHaye, The Act of Marriage, pp. 57ff.

[6] E. and D. Dodds, *Marriage to a Difficult Man: The Uncommon Union of Jonathan and Sarah Edwards*, Philadelphia: Westminster Press, 1971, p. 201.

[7] Although, I have also read the new book by D. Moore, *Good Christian, Good Husband? Leaving a Legacy in Marriage and Ministry*, Fearn, Tain, Ross-shire: Christian Focus, 2004, which includes a section on Jonathan Edwards.
[8] J. Edwards, 'The Wisdom of God Displayed in the Way of Salvation', in *The Works of Jonathan Edwards*, vol. 1, p. xlv.
[9] Dodds, *Marriage to a Difficult Man*, p. 78
[10] Dodds, *Marriage to a Difficult Man*, p. 80.
[11] Dodds, *Marriage to a Difficult Man*, p. 54.
[12] Edwards, *Works*, vol. 2, pp. 17–26.
[13] Edwards, *Works*, vol. 2, p. 21.
[14] See my article for further thoughts on Jonathan Edward's understanding of love. Simon Vibert, 'Remembering Jonathan Edwards' (Churchman 2003 117/4).

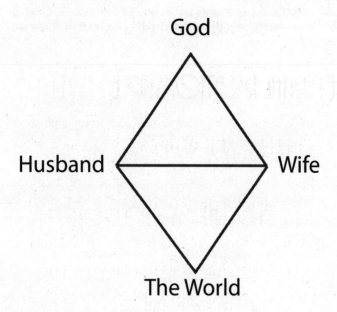

PART 3

BUILDING THE

ETERNAL RELATIONSHIP BETWEEN

HUSBAND, WIFE, GOD

AND THE WORLD

5

THE CHIEF END OF MARRIAGE

Working out the Eternal Implications of Marriage

I love hill-walking. My previous two church appointments were in the beautiful Peak District and just outside of the Lake District. In Wimbledon, you may have gathered, I now get much of my exercise and fresh air playing golf!

When climbing the higher mountains I find I get into a certain rhythm. At first the whole exercise seems impossible, but before too long, I develop a stride and dogged determination. After a while, the summit comes into view (assuming cloud hasn't blurred the sight). However, I have found myself deceived on a number of occasions, by the apparent proximity of the peak. Mountain tops seem close together until one approaches them, but upon arrival they hide a steep valley which needs to be crossed before the next summit.

Genesis 2 has a similar feel to it. Adam is looking for a helper. He is hungry for meaningful complementary companionship. None of the animals meet those needs. God intervenes to provide a unique partner in Eve, and now, it seems, he is happy.

But as we progress through the Old Testament, this is but the first summit along the way. God is Israel's husband, but Israel is a dissatisfied and wayward wife. But surely, in the church, the bride of Christ, now we reach the climax? However, according to Paul, quoting again from Genesis 2, we are not there yet. The summit is still in the future. We are only in the 'betrothal' stage. There will be a glorious day when there will be no more crying, no more loneliness, no more imperfection. On that glorious day, the wedding feast of the lamb, the unity of bride and groom will be a perfect marriage, a marriage made in heaven. The summit at last!

This makes sense of some important passages in the New Testament (see Matt. 22:30; 1 Cor. 7:21ff., for example). Marriage has a future fulfilment ahead.

It seems to me that many people don't see things this way. For them, marriage has become their only horizon. Many couples begin their marriage with a fairy-tale hope that their handsome prince or beautiful princess will rescue them from purposelessness and loneliness. The big vision of the household in the Bible has been supplanted by an isolated nuclear family. 'An Englishman's home is his castle', we say; and for some, the drawbridge is up, while they sit in front of the television in a home closed to the outsider.

Please don't misunderstand me, marriage needs protecting. The writer to the Hebrews intimates this in 13:4: 'Marriage should be honoured by all, and the marriage bed kept pure, for God will judge the adulterer and all the sexually immoral.' However, my concern is that many Christian marriages are lost in the fog of secularism.[1] They have lost sight of the summit to which Genesis 2:24 points. In the next chapter we will consider some practical implications of keeping the summit in view, but in this chapter we consider the significance of Ephesians 5:32: '"For this reason a man will leave his father and mother and be united to his wife, and the two will become one flesh." This is a profound mystery– but I am talking about Christ and the church.'

Peter O'Brien points out the double direction in which the text points:

> At one level, then Paul's teaching on marriage is grounded in the Old Testament while at another level the Church's marriage to Christ is prefigured in Adam and Eve.[2]

In Ephesians 5:32 Paul asserts that the true application of Genesis 2:24 is to be found beyond the relationship of husband and wife and in Christ's relationship with his church. Thus, by implication, the human institution of marriage is like an enacted parable, and a foretaste of that heavenly marriage. Hence, marriage is so key, because through it we can learn about Christ and the church.

This is the 'mystery' which we have already looked at in Ephesians 5 (see chapter 3). Paul's primarily concern in this letter is for the unveiling of the mystery of the gospel (see 3:8-9), and he sees marriage as performing that function too.

The Purpose of Marriage

My question now is, in the light of this theological theme in the Bible, what will Christian marriage look like? What is the purpose of marriage?

If the chief end of man is to glorify God and enjoy him forever, and if the chief end of God is to glorify himself and enjoy himself for ever, surely the same can be said to be true of the corporate relationship of husband and wife? The chief end of marriage is to glorify God and find in him and in their union, enjoyment for ever.

The dynamic interplay between the husband/wife and the church is instructive. Look again at how Paul interweaves these two themes:

Ephesians 5:25–33	
Husbands, love your wives,	Husband and wife
just as Christ loved the church and gave himself up for her to make her holy, cleansing her by the washing with water through the word, and to present her to himself as a radiant church, without stain or wrinkle or any other blemish, but holy and blameless.	Christ and the church
In this same way, husbands ought to love their wives as their own bodies. He who loves his wife loves himself. After all, no-one ever hated his own body, but he feeds and cares for it,	Husband and wife
just as Christ does the church – for we are members of his body.	Christ and the church
'For this reason a man will leave his father and mother and be united to his wife, and the two will become one flesh.'	Husband and wife

This is a profound mystery – but I am talking about Christ and the church.	Christ and the church
However, each one of you also must love his wife as he loves himself, and the wife must respect her husband.	Husband and wife

Everything that is expected of an individual Christian is now expected of the married couple. They are, after all, 'one flesh'. They act as one body. Just as the church and Christ are one body, so too are the husband and wife.

Practically speaking, then, we have already noted this application of the two Genesis passages which we looked at earlier in the book:

- Individually, the husband and wife relate to the world (they both continue to image God, Gen. 1:26f.)
- Corporately, they relate to the world as 'one flesh', one unit, one body, (Gen. 2:24)

When we see how Paul applies this Genesis 2:24 text in Ephesians 5, we will be closer to understanding the heart of the purpose of marriage. Human marriage points beyond itself. The purpose of marriage is not just to meet man's loneliness and provide him with a complementary counterpart, although clearly that is part of the purpose (Gen. 2:23ff.). The purpose of marriage is not just to provide Adam with a suitable helper in the task of tilling the earth and filling it with further images of God, although clearly that is a part of the purpose (note the context of Gen. 2). The purpose of marriage goes beyond both of these essential functions.

Marriage is a Temporary Arrangement

Shocking? Actually this is what Jesus teaches: 'At the resurrection people will neither marry nor be given in marriage; they will be like the angels in heaven' (Matt. 22:30). This is also recognized in the wording of the marriage service (BCP):

> I take thee to be my wedded wife, to have and to hold from this day forward, for better for worse, for richer for poorer, in sickness and in health, to love and to cherish, till death us do part, according to God's holy ordinance; and thereto I plight thee my troth.[3]

Marriage is only until 'death us do part'. It is temporary, time-bound, arrangement.

According to the key verse in Ephesians 5:32, there is something about marriage which points beyond itself.

> Marriage is a sign of eschatological hope. The festive mood at a wedding is a symbol of the joy and the fulfilment of human hopes that will be present at the end of time (see Mark 2:19ff.; Matt. 2:1–14; 25:1–13, etc.). It is therefore not simply necessary from the human point of view alone to celebrate the wedding as festively as possible, it is important to mark the occasion in this way as a hopeful anticipation and celebration in advance of the feast at the end of time.[4]

I would want to go further. This hopeful anticipation goes beyond the wedding day to the whole of the married life.

Walter Kasper also points out, there is a provisionality in the New Testament over the future of marriage (see Matt. 22:30, 1 Cor. 7:25–38). Marriage belongs to a form of this world which is passing away. Marriage is 'not an ultimate, but a penultimate and to that extent a temporary value… no partner can give the other heaven on earth.'

A person's urge to make such penultimate values absolute and his tendency to do violence to them can only cease when he recognizes God as the ultimate reality... The eschatological glorification of God is the final humanization of humanity.[5]

In passing we note that this is tremendously liberating for the unmarried person. The person who forgoes marriage for the sake of the kingdom (see Matt. 19:12; 1 Cor. 7:7) gives an eloquent testimony that they belong to the Lord and their betrothal to him will result in a glorious wedding on the last day. According to 1 Corinthians 7:28–32, there is a sense in which the single person is already married to the Lord, and to that extent, in a special way, they anticipate what we all will become in the next life. This also has important implications for the way in which married couples should relate to people outside the home (more on this in a moment).

In the life to come there will be no more marrying or giving in marriage. Many have pondered over why this is the case. Indeed, many a newly wed has thought about the frustration of spending an eternity, apparently, not married to his wife. Although, I guess for some, the fullness of the joy of heaven helps husband and wife work hard at their marriages now.

Why will there be no more marrying or giving in marriage in heaven? It is certainly true that there will be no more need for procreation, for heaven will be gloriously stuffed full of the children of God (see Rev. 5:9ff., for example). But surely, and more significantly, the passing intimacy which the human institution of marriage has provided will then be fully consummated in our marriage to God. This will be an event to supersede all others (Rev. 19:6–9).

The Eternal Dimension of the Diamond Marriage

This is how the bottom apex of the Diamond Marriage works out. Let me recap our journey so far

First, we began by suggesting that the horizontal dimension can be seen in the 'one flesh' relationship of intimacy and joy between the husband and wife. Marriage involves the process of 'becoming what we are'. In other words, in the public union of husband and wife in the marriage ceremony, they are made one flesh. The whole of their subsequent relationship involves becoming one flesh in their intimacy and communion.

Second, we have also seen that God intends this human relationship to be three-dimensional, not with the husband and wife in isolation, but rather with them submitting and loving in the same kind of dynamic relationship between Christ and the church. This will only happen when each of the marriage partners see Christ as the apex of the love-triangle of marriage.

Third, our task in this section of the book is to work out the eternal purpose of marriage. This is the very practical function of marriage, to be a visual aid, anticipating the full intimacy of unbroken communion with the living God, in heavenly union. We should rejoice in, and honour, the complementary nature of marriage because this gives eloquent testimony to the relationship between Christ and the church (Eph. 5:21ff.).

Our hope is that, as married couples see how they should relate to each other, they will become a visual aid, or a living parable illustrating to the world something of the saving love Christ has for the church. In human marriage we should see a heavenly anticipation, expectant of the full intimacy and joy of heaven, where there will be fullness of joy and the consummation of a perfect relationship with Christ (see Rom. 8:18–27).

It is in this way that the Bible expects marriage to be God's living, breathing parable. Paul reminds us that God made it this way. Indeed, because this instruction (in Gen. 1–2) was given before our forebears ever fell into sin, there is a sense in which *every* marriage, to a greater or lesser extent, gives eloquent testimony of God's purpose for the world (through their complementary relationship).

If this is the purpose of every marriage, how much more should it be intentional and practiced in the Christian household?

Marriage as a Living Parable

Building upon these principles, what follows are some practical ways in which we may help understand our marriage as a living parable. Here are five ways to rethink your perspective on marriage:

Think of the Church as an Extended Family and the Family as a Mini-Church

In his excellent book, *Man and Women in Biblical Perspective*, Dr Jim Hurley points out that the primary unit in the nation of Israel was not the family as we know it. The 'nuclear family' made up of mum, dad and two children is a modern, western feature which has become more standardized in the more recent past. Previous generations may have been more inclined to share larger houses with aunts, uncles, grandparents or unmarried siblings. Also, newly weds tended to live closer to parents or in-laws, thus extending the family.

Hurley points out that the family unit in the ancient near east was closely tied to other family units to form clans or tribes.[6] This meant that one God-given answer to loneliness was to be found in these extended family structures. Moreover, the specific instructions given to care for orphans, strangers and widows indicates that it is in this structure that God provides for those who are not married (see Deut. 10:18, 14:28ff., for example).

Carrying this over into the New Testament, we note that the church is called the household of God, or, the family (see 1 Tim. 3:4-5, Eph. 3:15). The church has a special responsibility to care for the poor and needy. The widows, especially, are commended for offering hospitality and generosity within the church (Acts 6:1; 1 Tim. 5:9–10). When we consider the notoriously badly behaved church of Corinth, we are reminded that it was made up of former sexual sinners, swindlers, drunks, gossips, thieves, etc. 'that is what some of your were', says Paul. 'But you were washed, you were sanctified, you were justified in the name of the Lord Jesus Christ and by the Spirit of our God' (1 Cor. 6:9–11). The household of the church is a place where sinners find a forgiving home.

Fathers are particularly singled out with the responsibility to bring up their children in the training and instruction of the Lord (Eph. 6:1–4).[7] And surrounding the instruction for all to honour marriage (in Heb. 13:4) is the very practical challenge to keep on loving the brother, the requirement to entertain strangers, and to remember and care for those who are mistreated.

The Christian's home is not his castle. Rather, a Christian home should be a place where men and women can experience the gracious care of God's people (more on this in a minute). It should be a mini-church where children are brought up knowing and loving God, where there is prayer, learning and imitating their parent's godly behaviour.

Similarly, the church should be a big family. We are particular concerned at St Luke's Church, where I am vicar, to avoid equating 'family' with 'nuclear family'. I often ask people to look around and notice the diverse ages, colours, genders and social backgrounds that make up the church family. We cannot call people to live kingdom standards, without providing a viable extended network of love, caring support and nurture, which should be the hallmarks of true church.

Families need to work hard at being church. Churches need to work hard at being family.

Continue the Task of Filling and Subduing the Earth

A little boy raced downstairs and said to his mother, 'Mummy, the minister said that "from dust you have come and to dust you will return" Is that true?' 'Why yes son, the Bible does say that.' 'Well come upstairs quickly, there is someone either coming or going right under my bed!' Fortunately the ongoing task to fill the world with more images of God is not dependent on reneging on our domestic cleaning!

However, the biblical mandate, 'Be fruitful and increase in number; fill the earth and subdue it…' (Gen. 1:28) still stands. I counsel couples to discuss the matter of having children before they get married, and then be prepared to revisit the discussion again after marriage. In our suburban community, I have also been quite concerned that many couples have so planned their domestic and social life that they pretty much plan when, where and how many children they will have. I am not sure that this is healthy and, though I am not against contraception, I do get concerned when it is merely used as a social convenience.

Part of the purpose of marriage is to provide the appropriate God-given environment to make more images of God. This does not, of course, mean that if a couple cannot have children they are not fulfilling God's intention in marriage. Neither does it mean that a couple should have as many children as they possibly can. However, it does mean that Christian couples should see this as part of the fruit and joy of marriage:

> Sons are a heritage from the Lord, children a reward from him.
>
> Like arrows in the hands of a warrior are sons born in one's youth.
>
> Blessed is the man whose quiver is full of them. They will not be put to shame when they contend with their enemies in the gate. (Ps. 127:3–5)

Biological Children

Recent family statistics have confirmed two things. The first is that the church is overwhelmingly made up of people who have been brought up in a Christian home. Yes, there are plenty of examples of people coming to faith from no Christian background. However, even if a child abandons the faith for a time, they are more likely to come back to faith through an evangelistic endeavour, than those who have never previously been exposed. Biblical texts such as the following, therefore, need to be taken seriously

> Fathers, do not exasperate your children; instead, bring them up in the training and instruction of the Lord (Eph. 6:4).
>
> Train a child in the way he should go, and when he is old he will not turn from it (Prov. 22:6).

Related to this is a similar point, namely that those who have been exposed to biblical teaching as a young person (through family and/or Sunday School), even though they may drift in teenage years, again are more likely to return to faith as an adult. Clearly the role of married couples is absolutely critical for the spiritual formation of children. This being the case, a good case could be made for arguing that the creation mandate for believers to fill the earth with covenant children is appreciative of the spiritual impact this has on the world.

Spiritual Children

Having established this principle, we now need to consider another important theological point which is relevant to our discussion concerning the fulfilment of Genesis 1:28. In the same way in which the household structure of the Old Testament has been taken up in the New Testament covenant community of the church, the Old Testament mandate to fill the earth is taken up in the New Testament 'Great Commission'. The role of the disciples of Jesus Christ is to go into all the world and make disciples of all nations. Consequently, as we continue to think about the God-given purpose of marriage, we must assume that bringing *spiritual* children into the world is a critical part of that role.

Once again, we note that the very things which are incumbent on every Christian (such as helping fulfil the great commission of Matt. 28:18–20), are also particularly applicable to married couples. First Peter 3:15–16 provide an excellent place to look at three principles which are relevant to this function of marriage:

> But in your hearts set apart Christ as Lord. Always be prepared to give an answer to everyone who asks you to give the reason for the hope that you have. But do this with gentleness and respect, keeping a clear conscience, so that those who speak maliciously against your good behaviour in Christ may be ashamed of their slander.

We note that this passage begins with instructions to a Christian wife who is married to a non-Christian.[8] Through their godly behaviour they may even win their husband to Christ.

First, verse 15a, Christ should be acknowledged as Lord in every area of the marriage and household (finances, childrearing, home-building, leisure, to name but a few). When this happens in a marriage, the outsider begins to ask the question: 'What gives this Christian hope?'

Second, verse 15b, they should consider ways in which they may be involved in testifying or evangelizing through their joint witness. This may involve offering hospitality in the home, using opportunities at the school gate and forming close relationships with other couples.

Third, verse 16, the joint witness of husband and wife should be characterized by gentleness, respect and a clear conscience. In other words, their lifestyle should match up to their profession. We live in strange days. Our 'politically correct' culture has very high expectations of marriage: complete equality and careful avoidance of any prejudicial language and behaviour. Yet at the same time, gender tensions continue to exist, and this often manifests itself in spoken or unspoken 'put-downs'. A Christian marriage should look different, by working out some of the principles we discussed in Chapters 3 and 4.

Clearly, these principles of evangelism are much the same for a couple as they are for the individual Christian. However, marriage offers corporate opportunities which may not necessarily be available individually. I can think of one Christian couple I know who have a very evident gift of hospitality. They are conscientious in including a wide variety of people when they host meals in their home, whether that be the casual Sunday visitor who is invited for lunch that day, or the single, widowed or other couples. There is no formal 'targeting' going on. Rather, they open their home to others, and inevitably as a result, conversations turn to Christian matters, as well as many others.

Model and Protect Your Marriage's Exclusive Singularity

A young girl was asked to describe what God intended when he brought Adam and Eve together in Genesis 2. The response read: 'God made the man and the women for each other and told them to stay married together for life. This is called monotony'.

There are two M's which characterize God's perspective on marriage, they involve a relationship between 'monotheism' and 'monogamy'. Let's take a minute to look at the biblical M&M's.

Christopher Ash helpfully points out the parallelism between the 'one God' and the 'one flesh' language. He quotes Karl Barth, 'The man who thinks it is possible and permissible to love many women simultaneously or alternately has not yet begun to love'.[9]

Monogamy

Monogamy is a necessity, not just for the health of society, nor just for the good of the children. Monogamy is necessary for the one flesh relationship to work. It is only by the total self-giving of one to another, in sickness and health, richer for poorer, till death parts them, that love may truly flourish.

Monotheism

Monotheism is a necessity for the same reasons. God brings his people into a singularly exclusive relationship, calling them to forsake all others, because there is only one God. Godly marriage, by its very existence, is intended to testify to this divine intention.

The late David Watson once commented, 'The man plays at love because what he really wants is sex. The women plays at sex because what she really wants is love'. This little truism contains some helpful hints about avoiding adultery and thus breaking the singular exclusivity expected of marriage.

A Word to the Wife…

To the wife, in particular, I would want to encourage you to realize that the man probably thinks about sex and love-making a lot more than you do. The apostle Paul hints at the waywardness of the human heart in this regard, advocating marriage as a way to deal with 'burning passions' which otherwise could be inappropriately expressed in sexual relationships outside of marriage.

I am not at all suggesting that the women should give in to her husband's every whim. However, Paul's counsel in 1 Corinthians 7 is that abstinence should be by mutual consent, in order for discipline and prayer, and for just 'a time' (see v.5 as well as v.9). Wives should not use sex manipulatively, nor should they automatically always resist their husbands advances. It is more of a physical appetite for him and the fact that arousal happens much quicker for him, and is a greater physical necessity, does not necessarily mean he is 'using you'. I think that men and women 'bond' slightly differently and certainly for most men, sex is an important part of that process.

A Word to the Husband…

The first thing I want to say to husbands is remember the wise words of Job: 'I made a covenant with my eyes not to look lustfully at a girl.' Jesus also warned that, well before the *act* of adultery, the *intention* of adultery has started in a man's heart. Note Jesus words in Matthew 5:28–30:

> But I tell you that anyone who looks at a woman lustfully has already committed adultery with her in his heart.
>
> If your right eye causes you to sin, gouge it out and throw it away. It is better for you to lose one part of your body than for your whole body to be thrown into hell.
>
> And if your right hand causes you to sin, cut it off and throw it away. It is better for you to lose one part of your body than for your whole body to go into hell.

Like Joseph in the Old Testament, sometimes we should flee situations which are dangerous to our marital fidelity, for what starts with an approving look, leading to an engaging conversation, can lead to bed all too easily – as all-too-many businessmen away from home can testify (see the account of Joseph and Potiphar's wife in Genesis 39).

Second, and more positively, may I encourage you to love your wife, tenderly, and all the time. The secret to happy marital sex, is often found in healthy breakfast conversations, romantic gestures, self-sacrificial duties, time priorities and real listening.[10]

Married couples who still love one another with an exclusive singularity at their diamond wedding provide an eloquent testimony to what God's covenant commitment with his people is all about.

Work Towards an Enduring and Winsome Faithfulness in your Marriage

The God of marriage is a covenant-keeping God who says, 'never will I leave you, never will I forsake you'. The couple who stay the course and remain steadfastly loyal to their covenant promises to each other, also witness to the character of God.

Prenuptial agreements and limited term marriage contracts are not wrong simply because they violate the biblical one-flesh principles of marriage. They are wrong, quite simply, because by its very nature, marriage cannot work under such circumstances. Only in finding oneself exclusively and enduringly committed to the other, will each find true and liberating love.

Christian marriage models this enduring faithfulness, which the covenant-keeping God shows to his people. In a day and age which has lost sight of the concept of 'my word is my bond', Christian couples will stand out in their steadfast commitment to one another. If for no other reason, we should be praying for, and working towards, the health and vitality of marriage.

Some practicalities may mean:

a) Resolving to only speak positively of one another in public, neither sarcastic or sexist in joking, nor deliberately belittling.[11]

b) Realizing that true love happens after marriage. We do not, in fact, truly know each other till after marriage. This is, perhaps, a particular issue which needs to be addressed when couples have been 'living together' prior to marriage. They may be inclined to think that by co-habiting they are 'as good as married'. However statistics demonstrate that marriage break-up is more likely to happen where people have co-habited. In part this may well be because they had all the 'trappings' of marriage with no prior intention to make a public lifelong commitment. When preparing couples for marriage in this situation, this less-than-ideal starting place needs to be addressed and discussed. These principles are just as true for couples marrying as virgins. You really don't know each other until after the wedding day. You do not fully know how your spouse will respond – in the bedroom, in the kitchen, in the living room – until after you have made a lifetime commitment to them.

Hollywood releases a constant stream of romantic films. As I write, one of the most popular films is *50 First Dates* starring Drew Barrymore and Adam Sandler. It took nearly $50 million in its opening weeks! The plot line stars marine biologist Henry Roth who finds his perfect woman in Lucy Whitmore. He falls in love with her, but the following day, Lucy doesn't seem to know him at all. Lucy suffers from a rare brain disease which overnight wipes out her memory. Henry realizes that, if he is ever going to win her affection, he will have to win her afresh every day of his life. The film is all about the inventive ways in which he tries to do that.

After marriage, many husbands feel that they have to shift from 'wooing mode' (through extravagant meals, leisurely chats, attentive listening) to 'providing mode' (long hours and stressful work draining any family time). This too can put a real strain on the marriage. Husbands and wives need to remember that the things which brought the couple together need to continues *after* marriage too. Men – woo her everyday!

c) Remembering that true love is shown when it is most unlikely to happen in normal circumstances (to the irritable, sick, depressed…). This kind of love is not the exclusive reserve of Christian couples, of course. But whenever it does happen, it testifies to the enduring faithfulness which is a mirror of God's love to his wayward people. True love is *agapē* love, as Ed Wheat points out:

> *Agapē* love is unconditional and irrevocable. God chose to love us first, before we gave Him our love in return, or even knew who He was. *Agapē* love gives without

measuring the cost or seeking personal advantage... *Agapē* love is not natural; it is supernatural... *Agapē* love has something both glorious and practical to say to the married couple, for it is this amazing way of loving *God's* way, which can become *our* way of loving by God's power.[12]

Appreciate that 'Wholeness' and 'Fulfilment' Belong to the Age to Come

Every marriage lives with this eternal tension in marriage. Every marriage has to deal with the consequences of sin. Every marriage should, therefore, be straining towards the full joy which we will find in heaven! This, after all was Jesus' perspective on his earthly work (see Heb. 12:2).

In heaven there will be no more marrying or giving in marriage, for the purpose of marriage will be consummated in the larger purpose of the marriage of Christ to the church. Everything which we have anticipated in part here on earth – joy, intimacy, security, communication – is taken up in the wonder of the heavenly marriage spoken of in Revelation 21:1-4:[13]

> Then I saw a new heaven and a new earth, for the first heaven and the first earth had passed away, and there was no longer any sea.
>
> I saw the Holy City, the new Jerusalem, coming down out of heaven from God, prepared as a bride beautifully dressed for her husband.
>
> And I heard a loud voice from the throne saying, 'Now the dwelling of God is with men, and he will live with them. They will be his people, and God himself will be with them and be their God.
>
> He will wipe every tear from their eyes. There will be no more death or mourning or crying or pain, for the old order of things has passed away.'

The practical implications for Christian marriage are huge! What an eloquent testimony and visible witness we will give to the world when through our marriages:

- people get a taste of what the church is really like;
- others can first hear and see the good news of the gospel at work;
- the world gets a picture of the exclusive loyalty which God shows to his people;
- we show sacrificial and enduring love, whatever the cost;
- we reveal a deep hunger and straining forward for heaven.

This is the purpose of marriage, and this is the very real contemporary challenge for modern marriages. In the next chapter we shall look at some of the practicalities of being a living parable.

---

[1] Secular = time bound in this world, this age (saeculum)

[2] P. O'Brien, *The Letter to the Ephesians*, Leicester: Apollos, 1999, p. 435.

[3] i.e. pledge loyalty, faithfulness. Taken from the Book of Common Prayer service for the Solemnization of Holy Matrimony.

[4] W. Kasper, *Theology of Christian Marriage*, London: Burns and Oates Ltd, 1980, pp. 42–3.

[5] Kasper, *Theology of Christian Marriage*, p.43.

[6] James B. Hurley, *Man and Woman in Biblical Perspective*, Leicester: IVP, 1981, pp. 21f.

[7] And in my experience often largely abdicate this role, unhelpfully leaving it solely to the wife.

[8] This is something that happened quite a bit as the church grew rapidly, however the Bible seems to be quite clear that it is foolish and unwise for any Christian to contemplate marrying a non-Christian. Paul seems to be addressing women who have become Christians after marrying, and their husbands are not yet Christians.

[9] K. Barth, *Church Dogmatics* III, 4:195, quoted in C. Ash, *Marriage: Sex in the Service of God*, Leicester: IVP, 2003, p. 253.

[10] Note LaHaye, *The Act of Marriage*.

[11] B. Hunter's book, *Being Good to Your Husband on Purpose*, Orlando: Creation House Press, is helpful here

[12] Wheat, *Intended for Pleasure*, p. 32.

[13] See Raymond C. Ortland, *Whoredom*, Leicester: IVP, 1996, pp. 164-9, for a helpful treatment of this passage.

[1] Contact: The Good Book Company New Malden, Surrey, or Scripture Union, London for two sources of popular Bible reading notes.

6

ΛN ENΛCTED PΛRΛBLE

In this chapter we will consider some practical goals which flow from our understanding of God's eternal purpose for marriage, and examine some the implications of Paul's application of Genesis 2:24 in Ephesians 5:32. In the Diamond Marriage Course, I teach both individual and corporate goals for the married couples:

1. *Individually* – Joy is found when any person realizes that heaven will ultimately answer the human longing for intimacy and companionship.

   Goal: To appreciate that, whatever a person's marital state on earth, they will experience true marriage in heaven and, like the angels, enjoy the fullness of experience with God (Matt. 22:29–31).

2. *Corporately* – Fullness of joy will be found in heaven at the marriage of God's bride (the church) to God's Son. In heaven there will be no more death, mourning, crying or pain (Rev. 21:4).

   Goal: To help husbands and wives appreciate that human marriage is penultimate, not ultimate, and thereby live their lives in eschatological anticipation of the completion of God's work.

Preparation Questions

- Have you ever considered the eternal perspective which the Bible spells out concerning marriage?
- Read these passages: Mark 12:25, 1 Corinthians 7:25–32, Matthew 22:30, Revelation 19:6–9.
- What effect might this perspective on marriage have upon your perception of your relationship?
- How might you encourage each other to trust God's ultimate purposes for marriage to be glorifying to him, when it is clearly implied that marriage, as we know it, will no longer exist in heaven?
- Have you ever considered your marriage to be a witness to God's saving purposes (see Eph. 5:32)?
- What implications might this teaching have for your relationship with those in the congregation who are widowed, orphaned or single?

Practical Implications

Marriage, Church and Being Family

We inferred from Genesis 2:18–25 that marriage was created as part of the divine answer to human loneliness. However, we also noticed that the complementary role of husband and wife is purposeful and not an end in and of itself. Moreover, it is clear that loneliness continues to exist both inside and outside marriage.

We should not underestimate the partial answer to loneliness which is now provided by God in the church family (see Mark 3:31–35; 10:29–31, for example).

We should also appreciate that marriage to Christ at the end of time will be the fulfilment of the human longing for fulfilment and intimacy experienced by married and unmarried (Rev. 19:1–9, 21:1–4).

- Do you have an 'open' home? Do you look out, especially, for the orphan, widow, single, divorced person?
- How can you protect the boundaries of your family and at the same have an open home?
- Have you got a pattern of corporate family worship? How do you plan to maintain this? Some suggestions below may help:
  o Use a scheme or plan for Bible reading – there are excellent resources available which can be done jointly as a family, or individually.[1]
  o Select a regular place and time of day which suites your temperament and routine.
  o Encourage prayer about both the big and the little things, and remember to recognize and thank God for answers to prayer!
  o Make the most of family meal times. Resist the temptation to take a tray in front of the TV, and perhaps extend 'grace' to include a more general prayer time.
  o Share the teaching and training of your children in prayer and Bible reading. Help them to see you adopt this as a lifestyle and habitual practice. They won't grow up doing it if you aren't committed to it.

Marriage and the Gospel

Consider your marriage's witness to the world around you. Do you feel equipped to 'give a reason for the hope you have' (1 Pet. 3:15)? Remember the implications from our study of this verse in the last chapter:

- First, Christ should be acknowledged as Lord in every area of the marriage (finances, childrearing, home-building, leisure, for example). When this happens it begs the question: 'What gives them hope?' Do you feel able to *answer* that question should people ask it?
- Second, you should think through ways in which you may prepare yourself for testifying or evangelizing through your marriage. This may involve offering hospitality in the home, using opportunities at the school gate, or forming close friendships with other couples. How can you foster hospitality in your home?
- Third, your joint witness should be characterized by gentleness, respect and a clear conscience. In other words, your lifestyle should match up to their verbal witness.

Alec Motyer has said, 'Lip without life, is hypocrisy. Life without lip is an uninterpreted parable':

- What do you think he meant by this statement?
- Which is the greater weakness in your marriage? 'Life without lip' or 'lip without life'?
- Is your marriage a 'living' and 'eloquent' parable of Christ's relationship with the church?

Train yourself to make the most of every opportunity which you have as a couple, to make Jesus known. Understand better the world in which we are called to minister. Michael Green summarizes the environment in which we live as follows:

- It is a world without God – at least , the God of the Bible does not feature in most people's thinking.
- It is a world without love – for most people, love is nothing more than a chemical attraction.

- It is a world without values – or rather, the values it holds, are arbitrary, subjective and relative.
- It is a world without meaning – people have little sense of God as the creator or it all, or of real hope beyond death.
- It is a world without freedom – the God of this age has blinded the minds of unbelievers (see 2 Cor. 4:4).
- It is a world without fulfilment – people are hungry for meaning and significance.
- It is a world without truth – there are no absolute standards to aspire or adhere to.
- It is a world without hope – whether this be global concerns over environment, famine, war, or personal directionless and despair.[2]

Educating ourselves in understanding the world which our friends, colleagues and family live in will help us in our witness.

- Do we speak naturally and unthreatingly about God?
- Do we show them the *agapē* love of the Bible?
- Do we hold consistent Christian values?
- Do we exude a sense of godly purpose?
- Do we shine with the light of the gospel?
- Do we offer them meaning to life?
- Do we take a stand on matters of biblical truth?
- Do we exude Christian hope?

Michael Green, similarly, encourages us to respond to the mental climate we live in:

- We need to live attractive Christian lives.
- We need to ask sensitive, probing questions.
- We need to suggest an alternative lifestyle.
- We need constant dependence on the Holy Spirit.
- We need constantly to build bridges.

Put into practice a plan to get to know some non-Christians. Quite obviously these relationships need to be fostered naturally. No one likes to feel like a 'target' for evangelism. And people soon know whether they are a 'project' or a genuine friend of you! Some practicalities may include:

Evaluate the key relationships in your life:family relations; friendships;work colleagues;recreational networks.Find ways to spend more time with these people. Inviting friends to dinner is always good. Become a part of the local community – neighbourhood watch or residents associations are good. Perhaps, invite the parents you talk to at the school gate to coffee during the morning. I like golf because I find it a good way to get to talk to non-Christian (and Christian men). Here is three-plus hours of uninterrupted natural, non-threatening conversation.

Grow in your confidence in sharing the contents of the faith with others. Look for natural opportunities as the events of the news of your Christian community come into conversation. Invite people to specific evangelistic events at your local church.

Marriage and Singularity

Adultery is a serious threat to marriage. The threat is so serious because:

- The world treats this issue so lightly
- The human heart is very wayward

Brian Edwards speaks of adultery as 'the act of breaking out of a marriage or breaking into another marriage; or separating husbands and wives by turning their affections away from their marriage partners.'[3] Consider ways in which you can prevent breaking into another relationship or breaking out of your own.

The Puritan writer, Thomas Watson warned of adultery in the following ways:

- It is a thievish sin.
- It debases a person.
- It pollutes.
- It is destructive to the body.
- It is a drain on the purse.
- It destroys reputation.
- It impairs the mind.
- It incurs temporal judgments.
- If unrepented of, it damns the soul.
- It destroys the soul of another.
- It is abhorred by God.[4]

Look at the positive and negative examples listed below. Take some time to read these biblical passages and discuss them together:

- Joseph and Potiphar's wife (Gen. 39):
  o How did Joseph deal with Potiphar's wife's advances?
  o Why did she react the way she did?
- David and Bathsheba (2 Sam.11, Ps. 51):
  o Can you trace the beginning of David's slide into adultery?
  o What other sins were committed apart from the act of adultery?
  o How does this warn you about the dangers of adultery?
  o Notice the specifics of his confession.
  o Notice also, the consequences of his sin, despite God's merciful forgiveness.
- Remember Jesus' words which condemn lust in the heart even when it has not gone all the way to adultery (Matt. 5:28)

Consider the following:

- What you wear – you must not cause another to stumble.
- What your watch on TV – particularly, remind yourself of the list of damages which Watson mentioned above, for TV will rarely portray adultery in this realistic light.
- Who you meet with – never in compromising periods with someone of the opposite sex; frequently for prayer and accountability with someone of the same sex.
- How you discipline your time – particularly, ensuring that you have a regular pattern of Bible reading and prayer.
- Your points of most vulnerability.

Michael Horton points out that when we commit adultery we sin against God, against our own body, against our spouse and against the partner's spouse.[5] Have you considered that avoidance of adultery includes:

- keeping our relationship with God healthy;
- honouring your own body;
- respecting your spouse;
- loving your neighbour.

Marriage and Winsome Faithfulness

Consider the ways in which you can mirror God's covenant faithfulness in your marriage relationship. Demonstrate practically that you are joined together in a covenant bond which illustrates God's commitment 'never will I leave you; never will I forsake you'.

- Be true to your word and keep your promises.
- Protect and build your marriage bond.
- Be rigorously loyal to each other, especially in public.

- Resolve to speak only positively of each other, especially when in public.
- Discuss ways in which the reality of 'true love' has become more apparent in the 'nitty gritty' of your marriage.
- Ask God to help you show the positive values of lifelong faithful love, and find ways to celebrate your love.

Marriage and the End of Time

Marriage is an enacted parable of Christ's relationship with the church. In so far as a marriage displays covenant faithfulness and self-sacrificial love, and builds 'one flesh' principles, it dramatically illustrates God's plan for the world.

To this extent a marriage will be at its most healthy when it appreciates that the future glorification of God in marriage will be fully manifested in the relationship between Christ and his church. Marriage is penultimate to the ultimate glorification of God.

I suggest that only this perspective on Christian marriage gives real hope for the future, and an appreciation that, even when death separates a loving married couple, they are able to accept that God is subsuming the chief end of marriage in a larger plan for his glorification and enjoyment.

- Spend some time considering the overlap between God's plans for the church and God's plans for marriage. How do you see biblical principles of headship, submission, and the glorification and enjoyment of God forever, worked out in your marriage and in the church?
- Read through Song of Songs and notice the covenant relationship between God and his people and the lover and beloved. How are the two relationships intertwined?

- How might understanding the penultimate nature of marriage help strengthen your marriage?
- Can you and your spouse identify periods in your married life when there has been the most tension or absence of joy?

Listed below are common areas of tension and stress in marriages. Grade the areas which are most likely to cause problems, or do cause problems at the moment in your marriage. I suggest you do this exercise separately and then discuss it together before the next session (no one else will see your responses).

Causes of Marital Friction

	LOW HIGH
Holidays	1 2 3 4 5 6 7 8 9 10
Time off/time alone together	1 2 3 4 5 6 7 8 9 10
Discipline of children	1 2 3 4 5 6 7 8 9 10
Communication	1 2 3 4 5 6 7 8 9 10
Distribution of domestic chores	1 2 3 4 5 6 7 8 9 10
Relationships with wider family	1 2 3 4 5 6 7 8 9 10
Love-making	1 2 3 4 5 6 7 8 9 10
Giving/receiving unconditional love	1 2 3 4 5 6 7 8 9 10
Money	1 2 3 4 5 6 7 8 9 10
Incompatible interests	1 2 3 4 5 6 7 8 9 10
Church involvement/attendance	1 2 3 4 5 6 7 8 9 10

As you discuss your answers together

- Did you notice areas where there are large differences from your spouse in your high/low stress scores?
- If so, discuss why this is the case.
- Can you work out some specific ways to help resolve the areas of high stress?

---

[2] See M. Green, *Evangelism through the Local Church*, London: Hodder and Stoughton, 1990, pp. 251–82. See also, J. Chapman, *Know and Tell the*

Gospel, New Malden: The Good Book Company, 1998 (New Edition)

[3] B. Edwards, *The Ten Commandments for Today*, Bromley, Kent: Day One Publications, 1996

[4] T. Watson, *The Ten Commandments*, Edinburgh: Banner of Truth, 1995 (first printed 1692).

[5] M. Horton, *The Law of Perfect Freedom*, Chicago: Moody Press, 1993, p. 188.

[1] B. B. Warfield, *The Westminster Assembly and its Work* New York: Oxford University Press, p. 397.

7

PUTTING THE PIECES TOGETHER

We began this book by discussing the problem of 'dutiful but joyless' marriages. We have tried to address this problem by looking at what the Bible has to say about joy and what the Bible has to say about marriage. Our particular focus has been on the biblical text, Genesis 2:23–24:

> The man said, 'This is now bone of my bones and flesh of my flesh; she shall be called 'woman', for she was taken out of man.'
>
> For this reason a man will leave his father and mother and be united to his wife, and they will become one flesh.

One of the key points we have seen is that marriage cannot be reduced down to a 'function', particularly that of procreation. Yes, marriage is part of the God-given structure and institution of a society. Yes, in Eve, God provided a suitable helper in the function of subduing the world. Yes, the creation mandate includes the command to 'be fruitful and fill the earth' (Gen. 1:28). But, the application of our text in Ephesians 5:32 points us beyond function to a future intimacy which we may enjoy with God – far beyond the passing glimpses we experience in this life. The goal of the Christian life is the consummation of our relationship 'in

Christ' – a future intimacy with God. Indeed the authors of the Westminster Catechism were surely right: *the glorifying of God and enjoyment of him forever* is our chief end!

It is worth noting that the answer to Question 1 of the shorter catechism ('What is the chief end of man?') is made up of two parts, and both bits are important, as B. B. Warfield points out: 'Man exists not merely that God may be glorified in him, but that he may delight in this glorious God'.[1] Warfield finds this theme in Augustine too:

> Thou has made us for thyself, O Lord: and our heart is restless till it finds its rest in Thee... Let God be all in all to thee, for in him is the entirety of all that thou lovest.[2]

Occasionally we come across marvellous examples of Christian marriage which have intertwined the glory and enjoyment of God with the glory and enjoyment of marriage, in a way I believe they should be. Kent Hughes quotes the former president of Columbia Bible College, Robert McQuilkin, who announced his resignation in order to care for his wife, who was suffering the ravaging effects of Alzheimer's disease:

> My dear wife, Muriel, has been in failing mental health for about eight years. So far I have been able to carry both her ever-growing needs and my leadership responsibilities at CBC. But recently it has become apparent that Muriel is contented most of the time she is with me and almost none of the time I am away from her. It is not just 'discontent.' She is filled with fear – even terror – that she has lost me and always goes in search of me when I leave home. Then she may be full of anger when she cannot get to me. So it is clear to me that she needs me now, full-time.
>
> Perhaps it would help you to understand if I shared with you what I shared at the time of the announcement of my resignation in chapel. The decision was made, in a way, 42 years ago when I promised to care for Muriel 'in sickness and in health... till death

do us part.' So, as I told the students and faculty, as a man of my word, integrity has something to do with it. But so does fairness. She has cared for me fully and sacrificially all these years; if I cared for her for the next 40 years I would not be out of debt. Duty, however, can be grim and stoic. But there is more; I love Muriel. She is a delight to me – her childlike dependence and confidence in me, her warm love, occasional flashes of that wit I used to relish so, her happy spirit and tough resilience in the face of her continual distressing frustration. I do not have to care for her, I get to! It is a high honour to care for so wonderful a person.[3]

This is a wonderful statement of true love, and worth quoting in full, I think. Did you notice his comment about duty? Duty alone would be enough to make him care for his wife. However, he realizes that delight makes him *want* to do it.

I want to spend a few minutes thinking more about some of C. S. Lewis' writing. I have already referred to C. S. Lewis in this book, however, as we try to put together some of the pieces of the Diamond Marriage, I would like to consider what he has to say about the matter of Christian joy.

C. S. Lewis and Joy

Unsatisfied desire reaches out beyond itself. In *Mere Christianity* Lewis speaks about a right and a wrong way to deal with our desires:

Creatures are not born with desires unless satisfaction for these desires exists. A baby feels hunger; well, there is such a thing as food. A duckling wants to swim; well, there is such a thing as water. Men feel sexual desires; well, there is such a thing as sex. If I find in myself a desire which no experience in this world can satisfy, the most probable explanation is that I was made for another world.[4]

This desire for another world is consummated in our glorification and enjoyment of the one true God. The God of heaven not only demands praise, but commands praise.

However, Lewis cautions, it would be a mistake to think of praise purely in terms of compliment or approval:

> I had never noticed that all enjoyment spontaneously overflows into praise.... The world rings with praise – lovers praising their mistresses, readers their favourite poet, walkers praising the countryside, players praising their favourite game – praise of weather, wines, dishes, actors, motors, horses, colleges, countries, historical personages, children, flowers, mountains, rare stamps, rare beetles, even sometimes politicians or scholars. I had not noticed how the humblest, and at the same time most balanced and capacious minds, praised most, while the cranks, misfits and malcontents praised least.[5]

If this characteristic is evident in human nature then it makes sense to assume that the praise of our good and excellent creator will be part of genuine human experience, even though for most people this stops short of its goal by praising creation, rather than the creator. 'We delight to praise what we enjoy' (C.S. Lewis).[6]

This joy and delight is something which will be consummated in heaven, where the angels even now are perpetually glorifying and praising God. In heaven there will be perfect expression of our delight in God and love for God: 'Our joy [will be] no more separable from the praise in which it liberates and utters itself than the brightness a mirror receives is separable from the brightness it sheds'.[7]

Commenting on the answer to the Westminster Shorter Catechism, question 1, Lewis concludes that we shall appreciate in heaven that the enjoying of God and the glorifying of God are the same thing. 'Fully to enjoy is to glorify. In commanding us to glorify him, God is inviting us to enjoy him'.[8] It is this interplay between our enjoyment of God and our enjoyment of our spouse that gives focus and power to Christian marriage.

This consummate end gives joy as a by-product and temporal foretaste of the heavenly, and does not find its complete reward in this life. This may be what Lewis had in mind when he wrote:

> Money is not the natural reward of love; that is why we call a man mercenary if he marries a woman for the sake of her money. But marriage is the proper reward for a real lover, and he is not mercenary for desiring it. A general who fights well in order to get a peerage is mercenary; a general who fights for victory is not, victory being the proper reward of battle as marriage is the proper reward of love. The proper rewards are not simply tacked on to the activity for which they are given, but are the activity itself in consummation…. If transtemporal, transinfinite good is our real destiny, then any other good on which our desire fixes must be in some degree fallacious, must bear at best only a symbolic relation to what will truly satisfy.[9]

Richard Attenborough's marvellous film of the book *Shadowlands* (1992) captures the love between Lewis (played by Anthony Hopkins) and the American, Joy Gresham (played by Debra Winger). They initially marry out of 'convenience'. Lewis wants to help her and her son escape a painful divorce from her drunken husband. They marry in secret. But in time he discovers he loves her. But this only happens after he overcomes his English stoical reaction to affairs of the heart. His Oxford academic colleagues are very cynical about his apparent slide into true love. He wryly remarks to one of them, 'How could she possibly be my wife, I would have to love her more than anything else…' Over time he becomes worried that in fact he loves her too much and that such love has an element of worship in it.

It is a marvellous account worth watching or reading.[10] However, his emerging relationship with Joy, earths the comments about love to God and joy in God which we see elsewhere in his writings. Reviving joy in our Christian life is essential if we are to live joy-filled, God-glorifying marriages.

Joylessness in the Christian Life – An Answer

In a sermon entitled 'Brothers Consider Christian Hedonism' John Piper outlines the reasoning behind his belief that our duty as a Christian is to maximize our joy in God:

> Christian hedonism aims to replace a Kantian morality with a biblical one. Immanuel Kant, the German philosopher who died in 1804, was the most powerful exponent of the notion that the moral value of an act decreases as we aim to derive any benefit from it. Acts are good if the doer is 'disinterested.' We should do the good because it is good. Any motivation to seek joy or reward corrupts the act.
>
> Against this Kantian morality (which has passed as Christian for too long!), we must herald the unabashedly hedonistic biblical morality. Jonathan Edwards, who died when Kant was 34, expressed it like this in one of his early resolutions: 'Resolved, to endeavor to obtain for myself as much happiness in the other world as I possibly can, with all the power, might, vigor and vehemence, yea, violence, I am capable of, or can bring myself to exert, in any way that can be thought of.'[11]

John Murray agrees that intellectual assent is not the same as heartfelt faith, and that performance of duty is not the acme of the Christian's response to God. The point is not that duty is wrong, but rather the problem is that disinterested duty has passed off as Christian faith, whereas Edwards, and now Piper, point out that the Christian faith has very much to do with the affections:

> There is no conflict between gratification of desire and the enhancement of man's pleasure, on the one hand, and fulfillment of God's command on the other.... The tension that often exists within us between a sense of duty and a wholehearted spontaneity is a tension that arises from sin and a disobedient will. No such tension would have invaded the heart of unfallen man. And the operation of saving grace

> is directed to the end of the removing of the tension so that there may be, as there was with man in the beginning, the perfect complementation of duty and pleasure, of commandment and love.[12]

Bible-believing Christians are often perceived as being emotionless, and characterized by joyless obedience. But the Bible assumes that those who are indifferent to their emotions are hard-hearted and sinful. This is what Jonathan Edwards has to say about this problem:

> Now by a hard heart is plainly meant an unaffected heart, or a heart not easy to be moved with virtuous affections, like a stone, insensible, stupid, unmoved, and hard to be impressed. Hence the hard heart is called a stony heart, and it opposed to a heart of flesh, that has feeling, and is sensibly touched and moved.[13]

It is wrong to be indifferent to our emotional reactions to God's truth, such an attitude is disobedient and not honouring to God. If I do not feel joy in life and ministry, then I should not soldier on, stoically, but, rather, I should repent! Piper's answer to the problem of joylessness (previously quoted) is surely right:

> [Do not simply] get on with your duty because feelings are irrelevant! My answer has three steps. First, confess the sin of joylessness. Acknowledge the culpable coldness of your heart.... Second, pray earnestly that God would restore the joy of obedience. Third, go ahead and do the outward dimension of your duty in the hope that the doing will rekindle the delight.[14]

This is borne out in passages such as Matthew 13:44, where conversion is synonymous with a seeking after joy. In Revelation 2:1–7, as we have seen, although commended for its faithful zeal and orthodoxy, the church in Ephesus is reprimanded because the Christians' love had gone cold.

We are not advocating that we should be pleasure-seeking hedonists in the way the world usually thinks of this term. To look to this world alone for happiness, fulfilment and joy, is sin. However, it is also wrong to assume that joy has nothing to do with the Christian life. Remember, joy is not optional (see Phil. 4:4).

The right response to God is to find our pleasure and delight in him. It is also true, however, that as we put our hope in God we discover that he 'richly provides us with everything for our enjoyment' (1 Tim. 6:17). Augustine once commented, 'He loves thee too little who loves anything with thee that he loves not for thy sake'. This, then, leads us from the more general subject of joy in the Christian life, to joy in Christian marriage.

Joylessness in Marriage – an answer

Duty is but a crutch until joy is revived. Joylessness in Christian marriage needs repenting of, and we should work at, and pray for, the reviving of joy. The unity of husband and wife in one flesh means that they now relate the principles of Christian hedonism to their corporate relationship:

> The Biblical mandate to husbands and wives is to seek your own joy in the joy of your spouse. Good done to the bride is good done to yourself because you are one flesh.... For a husband to be an obedient person he must love his wife the way Christ loved the Church. That is, he must pursue his own joy in the holy joy of his wife.[15]

You cannot exclude self-interest from love. The problem with marriage is not that we seek happiness, rather, the problem is that married couples seek happiness at the expense of one another, rather that *in* one another.

Commenting on the Ephesians 5 passage, Piper writes: 'Husbands should devote the same energy and time and creativity to making their wives happy that they devote naturally to making themselves happy. The result will be that in doing this they will make themselves happy.'[16] Because husband and wife are one flesh, if the husband desires the joy of his wife he will thereby be living for joy for himself. As 'one flesh' they are a new corporate human being, so married couples are to image God by showing something of his nature on earth now. Moreover, as husband and wife seek to work out their God-given distinctive roles, they give God glory and give themselves joy.

Joyfulness in Marriage Reflects Joyfulness in the Christian Life

In Hebrews 12:2 we read: 'Let us fix our eyes on Jesus, the author and perfecter of our faith, who for the joy set before him endured the cross, scorning its shame, and sat down at the right hand of the throne of God'.

This passage tells us that at the cross Christ loved the church in the one supreme act of self-sacrificial giving. Similarly, Ephesians 5:25 tells husbands to show the same kind of self-giving, self-sacrificial love towards their wife. The anticipation of joy motivates self-sacrificial love.

The second thing this passage implies is that at the ascension, Christ went to be with the Father, he was able to endure the agony of the cross because he was motivated by the joy that was ahead of him. Now, he is seated at the right hand of God in honour and power. Similarly, the married couple will endure all things for the sake of the joy ahead, which we suggest may mean enduring some things in marriage for the sake of the future reward of heaven. The whole Christian life has a 'now-but-not-yet' feel to it. The joy we experience in marriage is a foretaste of the fullness of joy we will know in our future marriage to Christ.

Next, remember that Hebrews 12:2 tells us that Christ is still waiting for the ultimate consummation of his love for the church when it will be presented holy and pure to himself, the work of redemption finally completed at the end of time. Then, in heaven there will no more marrying or giving in marriage, for the ultimate purpose of marriage will be subsumed in the bigger goal – the marriage of Christ to his church.

Finally, there is also a sense in which the joy of marriage is fulfilled now in the temporal relationship of husband and wife, which will be superseded by the greater joy of a consummated marriage in heaven between Christ and his church.

Don't be Indifferent to Joylessness

We have already discussed the fact that joy is not something that is tied to our personality or our temperament. Joy is a gift that God gives to those who make God their treasure (Matt. 13:44). And, yes, our treasures are mainly in heaven (Matt. 6:19-21). But, because of that joy ahead, we have joy now, in anticipation.

If your marriage is joyless, the right response is not to ignore it or assume that cold-hearted love is 'just the way it goes'. Rather, you should appreciate the great purpose of marriage and ask God to revive joy again. This is not just for your own sake, nor even just for the sake of your spouse, but also for the sake of your marriage's witness to the world.

I think that one of the reasons for the worldwide success of the popular book by Rick Warren *The Purpose Driven Life* is because the book encourages us to step back from the detail of our everyday Christian life and look at some bigger themes:

It's not about you.

The purpose of your life is far greater than your own personal fulfilment, your peace of mind, or even your happiness. It is far greater than your family, your career, or even your wildest dreams and ambitions. If you want to know why you were placed here on this planet, you must begin with God. You were born by his purpose and for his purpose.[17]

Knowing the purpose of marriage, even when that purpose is only fully realized in heaven, brings a sense of meaning and joy in this life.

In the play *Fiddler on the Roof* there is a very moving moment when Tevyev and his wife Golda are forced to move from their home in Russia. Tevyev turns to his wife and asks her: 'Golda, do you love me?' 'Do I what?' she responds. 'Do you love me?' Golda looks back at him and says, 'Do I love you? With our daughters getting married and this trouble in the town, you're upset, you're worn out, go inside, lie down, maybe it's indigestion.'

Again he asks, 'Golda, do you love me'. She breathes a heavy sigh and looks at him: 'Do I love you? For 25 years I have washed your clothes, cooked your meals, cleaned your house, given you children, milked the cows. After 25 years, why talk of love right now?'

Tevyev replies: 'Golda, the first time I met you was on our wedding day. I was scared, I was shy, I was nervous.'

'So was I,' she responds.

'But my father and my mother said we'd learn to love each other, and now I'm asking, Golda, 'Do you love me?".

'Do I love him,' she sighs, 'For 25 years I lived with him, fought with him, 25 years my bed is his! If that's not love, what is?'

'Then you love me?' Tevyev persists.

'I suppose I do!' she says.

'And I suppose I love you too!' he says, 'It doesn't change a thing, but after 25 years it's nice to know!'

It is a wonderful tender moment, when love between them is articulated, even though it has been very evident for years. Also, I love this scene, because Golda is able to move beyond the things which they do to and for each other, to focus on their love as being the prime thing, from which the things they do, flows.

Why Did I Write This Book?

Consider these two scenarios:

Jack and Linda

Jack and Linda are about to be married. They are both in their early twenties and very much in love. They grew up together in the church youth group, went off to the same university, and having graduated, they have settled in the local church, eagerly anticipating their wedding day!

They are both career-minded. Linda has recently qualified as an accountant. Jack is in management consultancy. Linda makes the 45-minute drive into a neighbouring city for work. Jack has a one and a quarter hour train/tube journey to London.

They have already put a deposit down on a small house. The house needs rather a lot of work, but that's fine! They will enjoy the time that that takes. They both have several siblings and their respective parents live at opposite ends of the country. They also have a very busy social life, he plays in the rugby club; she is a competent tennis player, and they have a lot of friends.

They both love Jesus. However, with all the busy social life, thriving career and extended family, there is little time to get really involved in the life of the church.

And now, they both sit, holding hands, eagerly anticipating their wedding day, on my sofa in the study. What do I say to this young couple? They are unlikely to need the minister to counsel them about their future sexual relationship and, anyway, I have two or three books which I recommend as compulsory reading in this department (cited previously).

If they were attending wedding preparation with me, my counsel would be along the lines of this book. 'Jack and Linda', I might say to them, 'you are clearly in love. I thank God for bringing you together. I do want you to spend plenty of time wooing each other and getting to know each other. I want you to learn to love each other with the same dynamic love that Christ loved the church and the church responds to Christ. But, I also want you to begin thinking about what it means to have your marriage as a living, enacted parable of Christ's eternal purposes for his people. Yes, even before you have children, can you make sure that you have an open and hospitable home where your love for each other is beginning to provide an evangelistic function in our local community? Will you do that?'

John and Anne

John and Anne are just about to celebrate their thirtieth wedding anniversary. They were married in their late twenties, and as they look at Jack and Linda preparing for their wedding day, they remember so many of those heady days when they were so obviously in love, setting up home together and beginning to plan a family.

They started their marriage with high ideals. And, when their minister cautioned them about the dangers of adultery, the problems of overcommitment, the pressures of bringing up children and looking after their household, they didn't really hear him. Yes, they knew the divorce statistics, but that wouldn't happen to them – anyway, they don't believe in divorce.

Neither of them *did* commit adultery, actually. But now, as they sit in their living room preparing for their grown-up children and grandchildren to come to their wedding anniversary celebrations, they look tired. They seem drained by the years of frenetic activity. And, now they have the added responsibility of Anne's rather frail mother sharing the house with them. There will be a big celebration but, actually, for them it feels more like an endurance test than a celebration.

What went wrong, they finally ask me, as we sit drinking our coffee? Maybe, if I may be allowed to give any counsel, I would encourage them to rekindle their first love. Now, before it is too late and they become completely set in their habitual reactions to each other, perhaps now, they should find some time on their own as a couple, doing the things which they used to do, and find time to relive the joy of relating to each other. Perhaps they could both find a special time to complete the Marriage Pledge form (found in Appendix 1) and give it to one another.

Maybe, if they do make this time together, their diamond wedding will be much more of a celebration?

The Diamond Marriage Course which I teach, and which is the basis of this book, has these two main audiences in mind.

Alistair Begg likens marriage to being like a plane journey. Long haul flights require a certain discipline. First there is the preparation for take-off, loading the plane and taxiing down the runway. This is rather like courtship and engagement. Then there is the take off itself, the great wedding day. Next there is the long period in the air – which is not called a long haul for nothing! Married life requires this long view. Finally, there is the closing stages of marriage, landing.

As a marriage preparation class, or for those who are newly wed, I use this as an opportunity to teach them about the bigger purpose of marriage. It is very easy to become insulated and inward-looking in marriage. We consider some of the dangers of the idea that 'an Englishman's home is his castle'. I encourage couples to let the drawbridge down in order that their homes are open and hospitable, and places where the gospel can be seen and heard. What a challenge for every Christian marriage to be that enacted parable, witnessing beyond itself to God's eternal purposes for the church.

I do have another audience in mind, however. The Diamond Marriage Course encourages couples to arrive at their sixtieth wedding anniversary still rejoicing in each other and finding their joy in their married relationship. This, too, is a wonderful thing.

One final golf illustration which has helped me in teaching this subject. I am relatively new to golf (and I won't even tell you my handicap!). Well-meaning friends have bought me several books on golf over the last few years. There is much that can be learned from books. However, I have found books on golf to be singularly useless. Yes, a few lessons have helped. Several sessions at the driving range have helped. But there has been no substitute for playing the game – regularly if possible.

So it is with marriage. Far be it from me to suggest that the whole of the foregoing is 'singularly useless'. However, I do believe that godly marriage cannot be learned from a book.

And I do also believe there is no substitute for time and practice. The only way to get your marriage handicap down is to put in the hours. Yes, occasionally it may be important to get the help of a professional. But, most of what I have to say about marriage is not difficult or complicated. It requires time, and a willingness to be a better spouse – for your good and their good – but primarily in order to bring glory to God, and enjoyment to yourself.

Some Practical Thoughts on Growing Joy

How does joy happen in the believer's life? Some thoughts for meditation:

Joy Will be Mine When I Know I am Accepted by God

And we know that in all things God works for the good of those who love him, who have been called according to his purpose... For I am convinced that neither death nor life, neither angels nor demons, neither the present nor the future, nor any powers, neither height nor depth, nor anything else in all creation, will be able to separate us from the love of God that is in Christ Jesus our Lord. (Rom. 8:28–39)

Joy Will be Mine When I Trust God Implicitly

I am not saying this because I am in need, for I have learned to be content whatever the circumstances. I know what it is to be in need, and I know what it is to have plenty. I have learned the secret of being content in any and every situation, whether well fed or hungry, whether living in plenty or in want.(Phil. 4:11–12)

Joy Will be Mine When I Realize That Heaven is Worth Everything

'Listen then to what the parable of the sower means: when anyone hears the message about the kingdom and does not understand it, the evil one comes and snatches away what was sown in his heart. This is the seed sown along the path. The one who received the seed that fell on rocky places is the man who hears the word and at once receives it with joy. But since he has no root, he lasts only a short time. When trouble or persecution comes because of the word, he quickly falls away. The one who received the seed that fell among the thorns is the man who hears the word, but the worries of this life and the deceitfulness of wealth choke it, making it unfruitful. But the one who received the seed that fell on good soil is the man who hears the word and understands it. He produces a crop, yielding a hundred, sixty or thirty times what was sown.' (Matt. 13:18–23)

Joy Will be Mine When I Conform to God's High-Pressure Cleaning

Consider it pure joy, my brothers whenever you face trials of many kinds because you know that the testing of your faith produces perseverance (James 1:2–3).

Joy Will be Mine When I Form Good Christian Habits

But the fruit of the Spirit is love, joy, peace, patience, kindness, goodness, faithfulness, gentleness and self control. Against such things there is no law. Those who belong to Christ Jesus have crucified the sinful nature with its passions and desires (Gal. 5:22–26).

Joy Will be Mine in its Fullness in Heaven

Let us fix our eyes on Jesus, the author and perfecter of our faith, who for the joy set before him endured the cross, scorning its shame, and sat down at the right hand of the throne of God (Heb. 12:2).

'For the Lamb at the centre of the throne will be their shepherd; he will lead them to springs of living water. And God will wipe away every tear from their eyes' (Rev. 7:17). To him who is able to keep you from falling and to present you before his glorious presence without fault and with great joy to the only God our Saviour be glory, majesty, power and authority, through Jesus Christ our Lord, before all ages, now and for evermore! Amen (Jude 24–25).

Spend some time reflecting on the big scheme that God began when he called you in his Son... this should change your perspective on whatever has happened this week!

Think about *all* that God has given you in Jesus... doesn't this help you be content in any circumstance?

The Christian life is costly – it involves giving up everything – but the reward is joy.

God doesn't waste circumstances, he uses them to make us more like Jesus.

The Christian life is a combination of saying no to our natural inclinations and yes to God's Spirit. The result is fruit that includes joy.

Heaven is worth the wait... fullness of joy will be mine forevermore.

Find an occasion to fill in the marriage pledge form (maybe on holiday, or on a special anniversary) and present it to your spouse.

---

[2] Warfield, *The Westminster Assembly and its Work* p. 398.

[3] K. Hughes, *Disciplines of a Godly Man*, Wheaton: Crossway Books, 1991, pp. 33f.

[4] C. S. Lewis, *Mere Christianity*, Glasgow: Fontana, 1981, pp. 104–5.

[5] C. S. Lewis, *Reflections on the Psalms*, Glasgow: Fount Paperbacks, 1987, p. 80.

[6] Lewis, *Reflections on the Psalms*, pp. 81.

[7] ibid. pp.80-81.

[8] Lewis, *Reflections on the Psalms*, p. 82.

[9] Lewis, *The Weight of Glory and Other Addresses*, pp. 26–7.

[10] B. Sibley, *C. S. Lewis Through the Shadowlands: The Story of His Life With Joy Davidman*, London: Hodder and Stoughton, 1985

[11] Desiring God website [www.Desiringgod.org], see also, Piper, *Desiring God*, p. 79.

[12] J. Murray, *Principles of Conduct*, Grand Rapids: Eerdmans, 1994, pp. 38–9.

[13] Edwards, *Religious Affections*, p. 46.

[14] Piper, *Desiring God*, p. 221.

[15] Piper, *Desiring God*, pp. 171–4.

[16] Piper, *Desiring God*, p. 175.

[17] Rick Warren, *The Purpose Driven Life*, Grand Rapids: Zondervan, 2002, p.17.

[18] A. Begg, *Made for His Pleasure: 10 Benchmarks of a Vital Faith*, Chicago: Moody Press, 1996.

RECOMMENDED READING

Christopher Ash, *Marriage: Sex in the Service of God*, Leicester: IVP, 2003. (mainly for leaders)

Alistair Begg, *Made for His Pleasure: 10 Benchmarks of a Vital Faith*, Chicago:Moody Press, 1996.

K. Hughes, *Disciplines of a Godly Man*, Wheaton: Crossway Books, 1991.

Tim and Beverly LaHaye,*The Act of Marriage: The Beauty of Sexual Love*, Grand Rapids: Zondervan, 1998.

Nicky and Sila Lee, *The Marriage Book*, London: HTB Publications, 2000.

John Piper, *Desiring God*, Leicester: IVP, 1986.

R. C. Sproul, *Intimate Marriage: A Practical Guide to Building a Great Marriage*, P. and R. Publishing,

E. and G. Wheat, *Intended for Pleasure: Sex Technique and Sexual Fulfilment in Christian Marriage*, London: Scripture Union, 1977.

APPENDIX 1 - MARRIAGE PLEDGE FORM

You may like to use the following pledge form on a special anniversary, or while away on holiday. It is designed to encourage both husbands and wives to recommit to some of the principles which we have covered in the Diamond Marriage Course. Further copies may be downloaded from the website (see Appendix 2 for details).

My Pledge to You

I _____ (name) pledge myself to _____ (spouse's name) in recognition of God's principles for marriage, to live as 'One Flesh'. From this day forward I shall make it my aim to:

- Leave behind things or people that hinder the two of us being 'one flesh' and work hard at uniting with _____ (spouse's name);
- Work out the principles involved in loving _____ (spouse's name) as Christ loved the church (or) submitting to _____ (spouse's name) as to the Lord (delete as appropriate) and do all I can to have the Lord as the reference point for all we do in our marriage;
- view our marriage as an enacted parable of Christ's relationship with his church and aim to so demonstrate my practical love towards _____ that our marriage may be a living witness to his purposes.

Signed _____

Date _____

PS (Anything else you want to say!)

APPENDIX 2 - RUNNING THE DIAMOND MARRIAGE COURSE

Dozens of couples have done this course with my wife Carrie and I, in our home, over the past several years. It has been one of the most fruitful of the small groups we have had based in our church.

The course is run over six weeks. Each week, there is a teaching component based upon the teaching in this book.

Chapters 2, 4, and 6 give the bulk of the practical exercises which the couples are encouraged to engage in. They prepare in advance for the next session by reading through the Preparation Questions. Then, at the end of the evening they are encouraged to do the Practical Exercises during the week, and find time to discuss the results with their partner.

On the final evening we share a meal together. The largest group I have had so far has been seven couples. This is probably a little too large. The only way a group this size works is if they split up to discuss the preparation question, so everyone has a chance to talk.

Building relationships with other married or engaged couples is a key component of the course, as some of the responses below, illustrate.

Six months after the end of the course we meet again for another meal and a chance to review the things we have learned.

One feature of the course, which I didn't anticipate, was the number of non-Christians who wanted to do the course. Where this is the case, I have adapted some of the evenings to encourage them to make a first commitment to Christ as part of the marriage preparation. I also take them through the evangelistic tract *Longing for Paradise* (see www.wimbledonchurch.co.uk/paradise/index). There are 10,000 copies of this colour booklet in print now, and it may be ordered from St Luke's Church, Wimbledon Park, London SW19 8DA (and at the website above). However, clearly the course is written primarily with Christians in mind.

The Diamond Marriage Course is not currently in print. The bulk of it is to be found in this book. However, we have also made available the text of the course at the website which accompanies the Diamond Marriage Course, available for free download (www.christianfocus.com)

Feedback Forms Completed by Participants of the Diamond Marriage Course
(Including some of the comments made by participants)

1. WHAT DO YOU THINK HAS BEEN THE CENTRAL MESSAGE OF THIS COURSE?

'God created marriage to teach us about him, and a godly marriage will relate up to God and not just out to the world...'

'Marriage is a practical preparation for our future relationship with God.'

'God is central to a good marriage.'

'The importance of good communication, and the significance of having a marriage focused on each other, the world, and God.'

'Learning to see our relationship in the context of God's plan for us.'

'For a successful marriage it is important to see the marriage as an allegory of the relationship between Christ and his church.'

'The need to place my partner within the context of Christ's relationship with the church.'

'Marriage is an earthly manifestation of Christ's love for his church.'

'To be united as one flesh and be more focused on the needs of the other.'

'Understanding that marriage is not the ultimate but God is ultimate.'

2. WHAT HAVE YOU FOUND THE MOST USEFUL FOR YOUR RELATIONSHIP?

'Taking care of the needs of my partner means my needs are met too.'

'Focusing on God in the relationship, finding time to pray, individually and together.'

'Learning from the experiences of others in the group.'

'Talking through the preparation questions together before each group.'

'Applying scripture thoroughly to our married relationship.'

'Appreciating our inherent differences and learning to celebrate and work with them.'

'Discussing issues with realism. Looking to the Bible for wisdom in dealing with them.'

'Taking time to talk about our relationship.'

'Seeing how our relationship fits in with God's plans for the church.'

'A reality check.'

'Being forced to have conversations which we would otherwise not have had.'

'Discussing the "Causes of Marital Friction" questionnaire.'

'Considering the bigger purpose for our marriage.'

3. WHAT BITS WERE LEAST USEFUL OR UNCLEAR?

Two comments here were:

'Some of the language and terminology was too technical.'

'Some of the questions were unclear.'

(both of which I hope I have now addressed!)

4. HOW DO YOU THINK THAT THE FORMAT, PRESENTATION OR STYLE OF THE COURSE MIGHT BE IMPROVED?

The main comments were:

'Improving the presentation and production of the course booklet.'

'More time spent in smaller group discussion.'

5. WHO DO YOU THINK MIGHT BENEFIT MOST FROM THIS COURSE?

Most of the participants so far have been newly weds or engaged couples. Hence, they felt that they would be the most appropriate participants. However I have also run this course with couples who have been married for longer, and they particularly pointed to the benefit of focusing on reviving joy in their relationship.

6. WOULD YOU RECOMMEND THIS COURSE TO ANYONE ELSE?

'Yes!'